MOOT COURT

WORKBOOK

D0146956

Aspen Coursebook Series

MOOT COURT
WORKBOOK

Finding Educational Success and Competition Glory

Suzianne D. Painter-Thorne
Associate Professor of Law
Mercer Law

Karen J. Sneddon
Professor of Law
Mercer Law

Wolters Kluwer

To contact Customer Service, e-mail customer.service@wolterskluwer.com, call 1-800-234-1660, fax 1-800-901-9075, or mail correspondence to:

> Wolters Kluwer
> Attn: Order Department
> PO Box 990
> Frederick, MD 21705

Printed in the United States of America.

1 2 3 4 5 6 7 8 9 0

ISBN 978-1-4548-7007-4

Library of Congress Cataloging-in-Publication Data

Names: Painter-Thorne, Suzianne D., author. | Sneddon, Karen J., author.
Title: Moot court workbook : finding educational success and competition
   glory / Suzianne D. Painter-Thorne, Associate Professor of Law, Mercer
   Law; Karen J. Sneddon, Professor of Law, Mercer Law.
Description: New York : Wolters Kluwer, [2017] | Series: Aspen coursebook
   series | Includes index.
Identifiers: LCCN 2017024228 | ISBN 9781454870074
Subjects: LCSH: Moot courts. | Legal briefs—United States.
Classification: LCC KF281.A2 P35 2017 | DDC 340.071/173—dc23
LC record available at https://lccn.loc.gov/2017024228

SUSTAINABLE FORESTRY INITIATIVE Certified Sourcing www.sfiprogram.org SFI-00756

About Wolters Kluwer Legal & Regulatory U.S.

Wolters Kluwer Legal & Regulatory U.S. delivers expert content and solutions in the areas of law, corporate compliance, health compliance, reimbursement, and legal education. Its practical solutions help customers successfully navigate the demands of a changing environment to drive their daily activities, enhance decision quality and inspire confident outcomes.

Serving customers worldwide, its legal and regulatory portfolio includes products under the Aspen Publishers, CCH Incorporated, Kluwer Law International, ftwilliam.com and MediRegs names. They are regarded as exceptional and trusted resources for general legal and practice-specific knowledge, compliance and risk management, dynamic workflow solutions, and expert commentary.

This book is dedicated to

My husband Matthew, my daughter Isabel,
and my father Joseph, who are sources of inspiration
—Karen

My husband Nathan for his never-ending love and support
—Sue

SUMMARY OF CONTENTS

CONTENTS   xi

PREFACE   xv

ACKNOWLEDGMENTS   xvii

CHAPTER 1   INTRODUCTION   1

CHAPTER 2   THE COMPETITION PROBLEM   11

CHAPTER 3   WRITING THE BRIEF   33

CHAPTER 4   THE ORAL ARGUMENT   89

CHAPTER 5   THE COMPETITION   131

INDEX   141

CONTENTS

PREFACE   xv
ACKNOWLEDGMENTS   xvii

CHAPTER 1
INTRODUCTION   1

A. Congratulations and Welcome to Moot Court!   1
B. How to Use This Book   3
C. First Steps   3
        Worksheet: Assessing Previous Experiences   5
        Worksheet: Setting Goals   7
    Chapter 1: Tips and Takeaways   9

CHAPTER 2
THE COMPETITION PROBLEM   11

A. Assessing the Problem Individually   12
        Worksheet: Issue-Spotting Checkup   15
B. Assessing the Problem as a Team   17
C. Recognizing the Record's Uses and Limits   18
        Worksheet: Draft a Client Biography   21
D. Competition Rules   23
E. Rules Checklist Before Writing   25
        Worksheet: Rules Survey   27
        Worksheet: Rules Checklist Before Arguing   29
    Chapter 2: Tips and Takeaways   31

CHAPTER 3
WRITING THE BRIEF   33

A. First Things First: Assessing Previous Experiences
    and Setting Goals   34

Worksheet: Assessing Previous Experiences
and Setting Goals   35
B. Collaborative Brief-Writing Strategies and Tips   37
Sample Schedule   40
Worksheet: Assessing Collaborative
Brief-Writing Expectations   43
C. How and When to Re-assess the Action Plan for Brief
Writing   45
Worksheet: Re-assessing the Action Plan   47
D. Researching the Possibilities   49
E. Theme/Theory of the Case Generation and Development   50
F. Using Narrative Techniques in the Statement of the
Facts and Beyond   51
1. Character   52
Worksheet: Character-Development Assessment   55
2. Point of View   57
3. Setting   58
4. Plot   58
G. Crafting Subtly Persuasive Questions Presented   59
1. Content of Question Presented   60
2. Phrasing   61
3. Structural Choices   62
4. Examples   62
5. Takeaway Points   66
H. Developing Winning Point Headings   66
1. Content   67
2. Structure   67
3. Number   68
4. Phrasing   68
5. Formatting   68
6. Examples   69
I. Summarizing the Argument   72
J. Organizing for the Audience (IRAC and Beyond)   73
K. Harnessing the Power of Language   74
1. Strategies   75
2. Example   78
L. Polishing a Winning Brief   79
1. Proofreading and Consistency   79
2. Formatting Tips   80
3. Using Checklists   83
Worksheet: What to Include in Your Checklist   85
Chapter 3: Tips and Takeaways   87

CHAPTER 4

THE ORAL ARGUMENT 89

A. Logistics and Structure of Oral Argument 89
B. Establishing an Action Plan for Oral Argument 92
     1. Preparing Your Case 92
     2. Preparing to Advocate 93
     3. Preparing to Open and to Close 95
     4. Preparing to Use the Facts 96
     5. Preparing to Argue 98
            Worksheet: Reviewing Your Arguments 99
     6. Preparing to Answer Questions 102
            Worksheet: Identifying Points of Conflict 105
     7. Preparing to Concede 107
     8. Preparing to Rebut 108
     9. Preparing to Use Cases 111
    10. Preparing Logistics 112
C. Beyond the Brief: New Arguments and New Research 115
D. Structuring Productive Oral Argument Practices 118
     1. Scheduling 119
     2. Judges 120
     3. Questions: Responses and Springboards 122
     4. Processing Feedback 123
            Worksheet: Sample Oral Argument Feedback Checklist 125
     5. Finding Your Voice 127
E. Team Management and Conflict Resolution Strategies
     for Oral Argument 128
     Chapter 4: Tips and Takeaways 130

CHAPTER 5

THE COMPETITION 131

A. Practical Considerations 131
B. Professionalism 134
C. Managing Stress 135
D. Processing the Competition Experience and the Competition
     Results 136
            Worksheet: Post-Competition Reflections 137
     Chapter 5: Tips and Takeaways 139

INDEX 141

C ongratulations on becoming a member of the moot court competition tradition. Moot court presents a unique and engaging experiential learning opportunity for law students. This workbook is designed as an accessible set of materials to enhance the educational experience of moot court and to promote both educational success and competition glory. The authors draw from their experience as professors who teach legal writing (including persuasive writing and oral argument), coach moot court teams, and judge moot court competitions.

Although this workbook will appeal to anyone interested in appellate advocacy, the primary audiences are law student moot court team members and moot court advisors. Students can complete this workbook individually or as a team. This workbook may also serve as a resource as specific questions emerge during the competition process. Moot court advisors and coaches may use the material as part of a moot court orientation or a course/workshop for student participants. Workbook topics are designed to advance students' understanding and use of persuasive advocacy skills without limitation to a particular competition problem. We hope you find educational success and competition glory!

July 2017

Suzianne D. Painter-Thorne
Karen J. Sneddon

T his workbook was made possible by the support of Mercer Law School. We are grateful for the support of the administration and our faculty colleagues. Thanks to the early reviewers for their constructive comments, suggestions, and encouragement. This workbook has been helped immeasurably by all of their contributions and we very much appreciate the generosity of their time. Perhaps most of all, we are grateful to the many legal writing students and moot court competitors whose experiences have encouraged us to create this book.

We appreciate the assistance of Wolters Kluwer and The Froebe Group in bringing this book into existence.

We owe a debt of gratitude to our families for their patience and support.

ACKNOWLEDGMENTS

conversation with the panel of judges mimic the practice of law, where briefs are filed and oral arguments held. Throughout the process, managing deadlines, collaborating with others, and handling stress are also part of the moot court process that prepares you for practice. The competition is a thrilling and stressful experience.

B. HOW TO USE THIS BOOK

This book is designed to help students maximize the educational experience offered by moot court. As highlighted above, moot court provides the opportunity to participate in a range of lawyerly skills, such as collaborating, scheduling, and managing stress, in addition to honing the skills of legal analysis, research, persuasive writing, and oral advocacy. The material presented in this book is designed to build upon your experiences in the required legal writing courses. If you have not yet completed the required legal writing courses, you may wish to review a legal writing text to gain a basic understanding of persuasive legal writing and the general components of an appellate brief.

This book is organized around the moot court competition, from reading the competition problem to assessing the competition experience. Specifically, this book will help you develop the brief and oral argument. These topics are designed to advance understanding, development, and refinement of persuasive advocacy skills (both written and oral) without limitation to a particular competition problem. Additional materials are available on the companion website.

C. FIRST STEPS

To begin, consider what you would like to achieve from the moot court experience. Assess your previous experiences, identify goals, and describe strategies that you may employ to achieve those goals. For example, the schedule you developed to research and write your required legal writing assignments may give you a starting point for the development of your research and writing schedule for a moot court competition. Reviewing feedback you received from your professors may help you identify which skills need further development and refinement. Looking at what you have already learned is the first step that allows for self-assessment and identification of your goals.

In addition, these questions can facilitate a conversation with your moot court teammates. In moot court, students work collaboratively in teams, each bringing their own perspectives, experiences, strengths, and weaknesses. An understanding of previous experiences can thus promote division of tasks and team harmony.

ASSESSING PREVIOUS EXPERIENCES

Before you begin a new experience, consider how previous experiences will inform and influence your choices. Reflecting on your previous experiences, respond to each question.

1. Define the word "persuasion."

_____

_____

_____

_____

_____

_____

2. To what extent does the definition of persuasion depend upon the context?

_____

_____

_____

_____

_____

_____

3. In light of your experiences, identify the characteristics of a persuasive legal writing text.

_____

_____

_____

_____

_____

_____

4. In light of your experiences, identify the characteristics of a persuasive oral argument.

_____

_____

_____

_____

_____

5. Identify the tools of persuasion.

_____

_____

_____

_____

_____

6. When considering the tools of persuasion, which tools are most effective? Explain.

_____

_____

_____

_____

_____

7. Most moot court briefs are written by two (or more) team members. What do you think would be an effective way to draft a brief as a team? Are there any challenges you anticipate in drafting a brief as a team? Identify any strategy you would employ to overcome such challenges.

_____

_____

_____

_____

_____

SETTING GOALS

In addition to reflecting upon your previous experiences, consider what you would like to achieve from your participation in moot court. In identifying your goals, focus primarily on the educational experience. That means that "winning" should not be one of the goals of participation in moot court. Don't get us wrong, winning is nice. The moot court experience, however, is richer than a mere win or loss categorization. As you formulate the goals, keep them concrete. For example, a goal of "writing better" is too general. The goal could be revised as "stop procrastinating on the writing process."

Writing in the space provided, please respond to each question.

1. Identify three goals, meaning three things you would like to know, learn, or experience as a result of your participation in moot court. Please be as specific as possible.

A. _____

_____

_____

_____

_____

_____

B. _____

_____

_____

_____

_____

_____

C. _____

_____

_____

_____

_____

_____

Now that you've assessed your previous experiences and identified your goals, it's time to describe strategies that you might use to achieve these goals. The strategies may include those you have used in your experiences before coming to law school, strategies you used in a law school class, or strategies you wished you had used in a law school class. As with the formulation of goals, keep the strategies concrete. For example, as a strategy to "stop procrastinating on the writing process," you may identify the series of tasks involved in the writing process and establish dates to complete those tasks that you will respect.

2. Articulate three strategies you might use to achieve the goals identified in prompt 1.

A. _____

_____

_____

_____

_____

B. _____

_____

_____

_____

_____

C. _____

_____

_____

_____

_____

Keep your lists of goals and strategies handy throughout your moot court experience. When you feel overwhelmed by research, argue with teammates about a citation rule, or are strongly critiqued by a judge, it can be helpful to remember your moot court purpose. This chapter was intended to facilitate your preliminary thoughts about moot court. Now, let's get to work!

CHAPTER 1
TIPS AND TAKEAWAYS

- Although moot court programs build towards moot court competitions, remember that the moot court experience is about more than winning a trophy.

- Use your previous experiences to set goals, and articulate strategies to achieve those goals.

CHAPTER 2
THE COMPETITION PROBLEM

At the center of every moot court competition is the competition problem. The competition problem determines the legal issues, jurisdiction, level of court review, and the factual record that defines the dispute between the parties. A thorough understanding of the problem is essential for advocates to present their best written and oral arguments.

A competition may focus on a specific legal topic such as criminal procedure, international law, family law, business administration, or Indian law. Or a competition may take a broader approach, with problems stemming from either state or federal constitutional topics that could encompass a variety of issues. Regardless of the legal questions presented by a specific problem, however, there are steps you can take to ensure your best academic and competitive performance. Your success—both competitively and academically—depends in large part on your mastery of the competition problem and your understanding of how that problem drives your written and oral advocacy. With that in mind, this chapter offers guidance on how to immerse yourself in the competition problem and strategies to effectively use the problem and competition rules to your persuasive advantage.

A. ASSESSING THE PROBLEM INDIVIDUALLY

Of course, the first step to assessing the problem is to thoroughly read the problem itself. The problem may be based on an actual case—either one already decided or still pending before a court. Conversely, the problem may be based entirely on a fabricated factual record involving actual legal issues. The legal dispute may be set in a real or imagined jurisdiction and involve state or federal law. Arguments may be held before a federal—or state—court of appeals, or more often, the U.S. or a state supreme court.

Despite this variety, most competition problems follow a typical pattern. The problem will contain a lower court decision that is being appealed to either an intermediate appellate or supreme court. It may also include a factual record. That record may rely on:

(1) The facts as presented in the lower court opinion;
(2) A fabricated fact pattern;
(3) Fabricated or actual trial transcripts; or
(4) A collection of materials in a fabricated excerpt of record.

In the first read of the problem, advocates should start with the facts. While starting with the facts may seem counterintuitive for practitioners, it provides students an opportunity to consider the facts without any preconceived notions or expectations that can arise if reading the facts with the legal issues in mind. Look at this review as an opportunity to identify any possible legal issues, much the way you would if you were taking a law school exam. Similarly, note any facts that seem particularly compelling or significant to the legal issues you spotted. Make a list of both legal issues and particularly significant facts.

After becoming acquainted with the factual basis for the dispute, advocates should read the questions presented for review as designated by the competition problem.[1] Because issues are often narrowed or streamlined for purposes of appellate review, it is possible the issues will vary from those identified by the lower court or by your reading of the factual record. For instance, the lower court may have considered and disposed of an assortment of legal issues, but the competition will likely identify only two issues for review. This is most typical in supreme court arguments, where the court will narrow the issues it will consider to those stated in the questions presented for review or in the order granting certiorari. Nevertheless, the issues as defined by the lower court or spotted in your review may ultimately comprise at least a portion of the arguments presented in the briefs and oral arguments. Likewise, those issues can

---

[1]Depending on the competition's format, the specific legal issues may be identified in a separate notice of appeal or briefing order or are to be gleaned by reading the lower court decision.

serve as fodder for research purposes and for generating arguments on the issues on appeal. Furthermore, it is possible that during oral argument a judge will ask questions about related issues or issues identified by the lower court or the bencher's own reading of the record. You want to be prepared to answer those questions.

Finally, read through the lower court decision, if one is provided.[2] In reading the decision, list any particularly compelling facts from the factual record relied on in the lower court opinion. Note any differences between the facts relied on by the lower court and your list of compelling facts. Don't discard or dismiss those facts that may have seemed obvious to you but were not included in the lower court's decision. It is possible those facts are compelling on the issue but were overlooked by the lower court or were discarded because they were contrary to the lower court's opinion. Indeed, those facts may be the most important in arguing against the opinion of the lower court in your brief or oral argument.

Moreover, in reading the lower court decision, note any cases or statutes cited by the lower court. Make a list of all sources relied upon by the lower court. Your research should always start with the sources cited in the lower court opinion, but it must also go beyond that to include relevant cases that relied on the same cases or statutes.

In reading the lower court decision, note the procedural posture of the case. The procedural posture may help you identify the relevant arguments for your brief and oral arguments. For instance, a decision to grant or deny a motion to dismiss will be examined differently by the reviewing court than a decision on the merits after a jury trial. Furthermore, the procedural posture may alter or determine the correct standard of review the appellate or supreme court will apply in hearing your argument. The standard of review, in turn, helps determine the relevant facts to include as well as what arguments may be plausibly advanced. For example, in considering an appeal from an order granting a motion for summary judgment, the reviewing court will assume that all the facts of the nonmoving party are true. That means you should not spend time arguing the veracity of the facts or evidence of your client's case.[3] Instead, your arguments should focus entirely on the matters of law before the court.

---

[2] If there is more than one lower court decision—for instance a trial court order and intermediate appellate court decision—be sure to read both opinions. Focus your attention first on the intermediate opinion that is the subject of the appeal. And note that the trial court decision may include resolution of factual disputes that may not be applicable to the legal questions in the competition brief or argument.

[3] Indeed, appellate courts rarely consider arguments disputing the lower court's factual conclusions.

ISSUE-SPOTTING CHECKUP

While reading about the lower court decision, list the legal issues articulated by the lower court. Compare that list to the list of issues you spotted when reading the factual record.

1. Identify any issue the lower court discussed that you did not identify in your review of the record:

_____

_____

_____

_____

_____

_____

_____

2. Identify any issue you identified in your review of the record that the lower court did not consider:

_____

_____

_____

_____

_____

_____

_____

This exercise can help you assess your issue-spotting skills, which are critical for a lawyer to possess. Do not be discouraged if you have spotted different issues or a greater number of issues than those relied on by the lower court. Instead, consider what, if anything, you may have missed in your read-through. You might have missed an issue because it concerns an unfamiliar area of law or because your reading of the material was not as close or attentive as it should be. On the other hand, if you spotted issues that were not considered by the lower court, it may be that you fell for red herrings or spotted insignificant issues that would be unlikely to receive appellate or Supreme Court review. Practice is not like a law school exam where you are rewarded for spotting every issue. It is more narrowly focused to those issues that are sufficiently complex to justify the costs of legal services. Nonetheless, your exercise in issue spotting can help with your own research and argument development even if you spot issues that go beyond those presented by the court.[4]

B. ASSESSING THE PROBLEM AS A TEAM

Typically, the competition problem consists of two legal questions. The practical reason for this is that two issues allow teams of two members to more neatly divide oral argument during competition. In some competition problems, the issues presented involve two distinct bases for legal decision-making. In those circumstances, dividing the issues between a two-member team is relatively easy. However, in other instances, the legal issues may overlap or involve similar questions. Assessing the problem as a team during the brief-writing process will help in the future with the oral arguments. For instance, a problem may involve an issue implicating procedural and substantive arguments on the same topic. It is those circumstances that can create headaches for advocates, as demarcating a clear line between the two arguments can be challenging. This is particularly so in oral arguments, where advocates are likely to get questions that more properly should be directed at a teammate. This is not to suggest that a misdirected question may not occur when there are two independent bases of argument. Indeed, given the pace of oral arguments, it is possible—even likely—that a judge will get so caught up in the argument that she or he will direct a question on the wrong issue to the wrong advocate. But it is more likely to happen the more closely linked the two issues appear to be.

Furthermore, advocates must understand both legal issues involved because decisions regarding one issue might affect the validity or

---

[4]For more on this topic, see Chapter 4, section C, Beyond the Brief: New Arguments and New Research.

credibility of arguments on the other issue. When issues overlap, it is possible that a decision on one issue might undermine the position a teammate is taking. Being aware of the issues during the research and argument formulation may help you decide as a team if one issue is worth conceding. Attorneys often argue in the alternative and most experienced lawyers understand that an attorney who concedes defeat on one independent legal basis has not abandoned the other. However, in moot court competitions both advocates are expected to be equal. Because each advocate's argument is necessary to accumulate team points for the purpose of the competition, it is not desirable to concede an entire issue. Thus, you must find ways to argue both issues without undermining the other—both in your written briefs and during oral argument.

While the structure of the competition problem may encourage—and even demand—a division of topic by advocate, each advocate must be well versed in their teammate's arguments and positions. There are several ways to ensure this competency. First, before drafting, advocates should brainstorm and map out the arguments to be made on all the issues. Each team member should read the major cases for each other's arguments. Share notes taken from your individual reading of the problem with your teammate. Share your thoughts and notes on the major cases and the arguments they support or undermine. Together, generate a list of arguments for both issues and agree to a ranking of the arguments in terms of their persuasive value and relevance. Look for common threads in all the arguments, which can help generate a unified theme to use in the brief or in oral argument.

Second, in drafting the brief, advocates should collaborate in writing all of its parts. Often advocates will divide writing the argument section by legal issue. If, however, both advocates work to research and draft both issues, they will consequently come to understand the arguments to be made more thoroughly. Even if drafting will not be done collaboratively, it should at a minimum be done with regular consultation between teammates. Throughout the drafting process, continue to discuss the issues with your teammate and use each other as sounding boards to test arguments and theories. Schedule regular meetings—by phone, email, messages, or even in person—to provide updates and seek feedback.[5]

C. RECOGNIZING THE RECORD'S USES AND LIMITS

In drafting briefs and preparing for oral argument, advocates must consider how to strategically use the record. Generally, advocates should

---

[5]Collaborative brief-writing strategies will be discussed in Chapter 3.

expect to remain within the competition record. With the exception of judicial notice, reviewing courts are typically limited to the facts as presented in the record developed in the lower court. That means that any fact that is not in the competition record simply does not exist for the purposes of that competition. However, that does not mean every fact can be found on the written page. Indeed, part of your strategic use of the record includes considering what, if any, relevant facts are not contained in the record. A fact that is missing from the record may form the basis for a useful distinction from a precedent case. A missing fact may demonstrate the failure to meet an evidentiary or persuasive burden on a required element. Thus, advocates should compile a list of any seemingly "missing" facts. However, be careful in making assumptions about what is not included in the record. Just because a fact was important in a precedent case, its absence in your case's record does not necessarily make the precedent case entirely inapplicable.

As suggested above,[6] in your first reading of the problem, you should have taken notes of any facts you thought might be particularly relevant. However, do not limit your use of the facts to only those that support your arguments. Rather, any facts that included in the lower court decision should be considered in your brief—either to support your contentions or to explain why they do not compel the result reached by the lower court. Similarly, as you research your legal arguments, return to the factual record—you may find that facts that seemed irrelevant are suddenly vitally important as your research uncovers new cases and as you further develop your arguments. Finally, during oral argument practice rounds, questions from the bench may implicate facts you may have overlooked. Consequently, throughout all stages of competition preparation, advocates should continue to refer to and update their understanding of the factual record. That means advocates must never assume they know the record well enough. Instead, plan to read and re-read the record multiple times throughout the brief-writing and oral argument preparation stages.

Nevertheless, in selecting their strategy, advocates are not typically limited to the facts as stated in the lower court's opinion (unless stated otherwise in the competition rules, or if the competition has no separate factual record other than the lower court opinion). The lower court opinion was written with the goal of supporting the lower court's reasoning. But the goals of your brief and oral argument will differ. In the appeals process, one side will argue for a contrary conclusion from that reached by the lower court, which can implicate different or additional facts from those relied upon by the lower court. Furthermore, even the party seeking to uphold the lower court's decision may find that additional facts are relevant given the specific issues raised on the appeal or the particular

---

[6] Section A. Assessing the Problem Individually.

arguments being advanced in the brief. Thus, you should not rely upon only those facts presented in the lower court decision unless that decision is the only basis for the competition record.

Typically, the legal issues on appeal determine which facts are relevant. That is because advocates argue those facts that compel a particular result on a particular legal issue. Consequently, it can be easy to ignore other facts that can be equally persuasive. For instance, advocates should consider how to best integrate important background facts—that is, those facts that are not relevant to the legal arguments but are necessary to understand the client or have the complete context of the facts under which the dispute arose. Background facts serve another useful purpose unique to moot court competitions. Just like law school exams, moot court competitions do not involve live clients. Student advocates—and competition judges—can find it difficult to relate to a client who exists only on paper. Nevertheless, part of effective advocacy is believing in the client's cause, which can often mean understanding the client's motivations and point of view. To do that, you need to create a client from the facts on the paper. Primarily that is done by looking at the background facts, which tend to focus on the history and life of your paper client. Using the facts to humanize the client can help advocates and judges relate to the client as a "person" and thereby demonstrate a sincere concern for the issues during argument. It can also help persuade the bench that the advocates' cause is just.

DRAFT A CLIENT BIOGRAPHY

After reading the record, draft a biography of your client. To start that process, identify:

1. Your client's name:

_____

_____

_____

_____

_____

2. Any unique characteristics about your client:

_____

_____

_____

_____

_____

3. Your client's ideal outcome:

_____

_____

_____

_____

_____

4. Your client's motivation in pursuing this appeal:

_____

_____

_____

_____

_____

5. Any hardships faced by your client:

_____

_____

_____

_____

_____

6. Any good fortune experienced by your client:

_____

_____

_____

_____

_____

7. The non-legal outcome your client really desires:

_____

_____

_____

_____

_____

WORKSHEET

D. COMPETITION RULES

Apart from the obvious step of thoroughly reading the problem, advocates should closely consider the competition's rules and how they affect the competition's structure and arguments. Keep in mind that the competition's rules might differ from those you learned in your legal writing class or through a judicial externship. Indeed, they will likely differ from the rules enforced in federal and state courts. Even the competition rules for problems set in the U.S. Supreme Court will differ from those of the actual Court. Nevertheless, the need to respect the local rules in moot court is just as essential to a moot court advocate's success as it is in a real courtroom.

Generally, competition rules dictate how the record may be used in the advocates' briefs and oral argument rounds, the sources that may be consulted in conducting research, the structure of the advocates' briefs, and the composition of oral arguments. But more than that, the rules set the parameters of the competition problem and help guide the advocates' brief drafting and argument preparation. Rather than looking at the rules as restrictions on effective advocacy, advocates should seek a thorough understanding of the rules so that they may more effectively work within the limits set by them.

Competition rules will determine what sources may—or may not—be consulted in preparing briefs or arguments. For instance, a competition that uses a pending Supreme Court case may prohibit advocates from consulting briefs filed by the real life advocates. Conversely, the rules may make those briefs part of the official record of the competition. Likewise, a problem set in a fictional jurisdiction that also relies on a pending court case may deem "real life" materials as outside the scope of the record or problem. Even if the rules permit the use of real life materials, they may only permit those materials for use as part of the factual record while prohibiting advocates from consulting the legal arguments advanced in those briefs. For instance, it is not uncommon for competition problems based on pending Supreme Court issues to prohibit advocates from listening to the oral arguments from the filed case.

To the extent the competition problem and the real world basis for that problem differ, advocates should stick to the competition record. Unless the competition expressly makes the actual briefs and records part of the competition problem, you should not assume that an issue or fact in the real-world case will be applicable to the competition problem. Indeed, some issues or facts may have been changed for the purposes of creating more streamlined or competition-friendly legal issues. Over-reliance on the real world record could lead you astray by suggesting issues or facts in the competition problem that do not exist in the competition's universe.

Moreover, competitions may impose other limits regardless of the source of the competition problem. Many competitions prohibit advocates from receiving assistance from anyone who is not a member of their team. Such a rule means that advocates may not consult with classmates, faculty members, or their team coaches in crafting arguments or in drafting their briefs. For some competitions, this rule carries over into practice rounds for oral argument; for others, it applies only to the written brief. If there is any confusion regarding what sources may be consulted, advocates should seek clarification with the competition host before the deadline, rather than risk a rule infraction. Be sure to check the competition webpage for updates and rule clarifications.

Just like local court rules, competition rules also govern many of the details of the brief. These details include what citation manual to use, the typeface, sections of the brief to include, and the writer's freedom to re-draft questions presented in the competition problem. If the rules do allow you to re-draft the questions presented, embrace the opportunity to present the issue in a way that is persuasive for your client. It is an opportunity to incorporate your brief's theme.

Furthermore, the rules will specify the required sections of the brief as well as the order in which those sections should be presented. These sections and rules may differ from those required by your legal writing professor.[7] Thus, competitors should not assume that competition briefs will use the same format and should not rely on templates or checklists from their legal writing class in drafting competition briefs. Instead, as discussed later in Chapter 3, you should review the competition rules and craft your own checklist to ensure that your brief conforms to these rules.

In presenting arguments in the written brief, the competition rules will set page limits and may provide other restrictions on the manner in which arguments may be presented. In considering the page limits, team members will need to agree on an appropriate division of the available number of pages. It can be easy to assume that both issues deserve the same number of pages. That assumption may be incorrect, however. Instead, advocates will have to consider the relative complexity of the two issues presented and the relative merits and strengths of the arguments to be made in allocating page resources. More complex issues may need more pages to convey the entirety of the argument. Similarly, you will want to focus the court's attention on the brief's stronger arguments by providing more detail on those arguments. That increased detail will necessarily increase the length of the argument on that issue. Furthermore, advocates must consider that a brief is more than just the argument section. Thus, the argument should not comprise the entire page limit, as you will need to include a statement of facts, questions presented, and other sections.

---

[7]The specific competition rules will also determine many of the details, such as formatting requirements, which are discussed in Chapter 3.

Flexibility throughout the writing process is always critical, but especially when working as part of a team. Staying flexible may be challenging, as each advocate will often want to highlight her or his arguments. However, success in moot court—and in life—depends on the shared success of the team more than that of either individual member. Thus, plan to re-assess the brief throughout the research and writing process. For instance, avoid setting the allocation of brief space too early in the process before your arguments are fully developed. Setting limits too early may result in a less than ideal distribution once the legal issues have been thoroughly researched. Indeed, once research is completed, you may find that some issues will take more time to explain or that other issues are less persuasive and thereby less deserving of attention in the brief. But once the drafts have been written, it can be difficult to envision a different division. Nevertheless, an overly rigid enforcement of the division of pages may result in a complex issue not receiving sufficient attention, while a more straightforward issue receives too much detail simply as a device to meet the page limit. Both possibilities can undermine your arguments by suggesting that you were not able to discern their relative value. Moreover, focusing too much detail on a weaker argument risks exposing its flaws. Similarly, curt treatment of a compelling issue undercuts the opportunity to use detail as a method to focus the reader on the stronger part of your brief. Of course, it is equally true that waiting too late to set the limit means writing without the guidance that page limits provide. It's a truism that "work expands to fill the space," and that is particularly true in legal writing. Page limits help set the limits of that space, and can force advocates to concisely hone in on the strongest arguments. Thus, rather than set a firm page limit, you should set a range for each argument. Agree to re-assess the limits throughout the drafting process and to adjust accordingly.

E. RULES CHECKLIST BEFORE WRITING

As you read the competition rules, keep in mind that the rules will affect your final brief in several ways. They will surely designate a page or word limit for the entire brief and may include limits on each argument. The rules will determine the required parts of the brief and the order in which the parts must appear. The rules may require a particular citation format. And of course, the rules will determine how much time you have to complete your competition brief.

RULES SURVEY

Before writing the brief, it is important to identify the ways in which the rules will affect your approach. Identify the following:

1. Final brief deadline:

_____

_____

_____

_____

_____

_____

_____

2. Page or word limit for the brief or any parts of the brief:

_____

_____

_____

_____

_____

_____

3. Formatting requirements, including (a) page size, (b) text spacing, and (c) font and type size requirements:

_____

_____

_____

_____

_____

_____

_____

WORKSHEET

WORKSHEET

4. Sections of the brief that must be included:

_____

_____

_____

_____

_____

_____

_____

5. Citation manual or format required:

_____

_____

_____

_____

_____

_____

_____

RULES CHECKLIST BEFORE ARGUING

In much the same way the competition rules will affect your approach to brief writing, you should use the rules to guide your preparation for oral argument. In reviewing the rules, identify the following:

1. Time limit on overall argument:

_____

_____

_____

_____

_____

_____

_____

2. Time limit on individual argument:

_____

_____

_____

_____

_____

_____

_____

3. Amount of time permitted for rebuttal:

_____

_____

_____

_____

_____

_____

_____

WORKSHEET

4. Whether sur-rebuttal is permitted and the amount of time allowed:

_____

_____

_____

_____

_____

_____

_____

5. Whether one team must deliver rebuttal:

_____

_____

_____

_____

_____

_____

_____

WORKSHEET

CHAPTER 2
TIPS AND TAKEAWAYS

■ Review the competition rules to determine the limits and uses of the competition record.

■ Plan to review the competition problem multiple times during the competition preparation process.

■ Read the competition record strategically to isolate the legal issues, identify the critical facts, and recognize key policy considerations.

CHAPTER 3
WRITING THE BRIEF

While those new to moot court tend to imagine moot court competitions as being rounds of oral arguments before dispassionate judges, the competition actually starts with the drafting of the competition brief. Indeed, the competition brief is the cornerstone of every moot court competition. It is the first component of the competition completed by the competitors. It is the first place for competitors to present their arguments. And it is the foundation for oral arguments. At the competition, the appellate brief is also relevant. For instance, prizes are awarded for best petitioner's brief and best respondent's brief. In addition, brief scores affect advancement at the competition. The brief scores are often calculated with the oral argument round scores to determine which team advances to the next round. Thus, the competition brief—and the score the brief received—may ultimately determine which team wins any particular competition. Consequently, the competition brief is critical to your moot court performance. More importantly, writing the brief is an opportunity to learn—which is what moot court is really about.

Much of what is required for a moot court brief you will have learned in your law school course on persuasive writing. How to use persuasive language, how to present authorities, how to argue using facts, and how to divide the argument into different parts are all implicated in writing a competition brief. This chapter will build upon that foundation to reinforce key points and to share advanced techniques.

Nevertheless, writing a competition brief can present unique challenges not implicated in standard law school legal writing courses. The primary challenge is that few competitions allow for feedback or guidance from faculty members or writing specialists. Furthermore, unlike in most writing courses, student competitors draft their brief as part of a team, which requires collaboration with one or more teammates. Moreover, while courses in persuasive writing typically focus on drafting trial or appellate briefs, most moot court competitions involve supreme court briefs, which differ from intermediate appellate briefs in important ways.

Accordingly, this section will provide advice on planning and drafting the competition brief. It will begin with a general overview of the collaborative nature of the brief-writing process. It will discuss the scheduling process, from identifying the issues to submitting the final brief. A sample schedule with deadlines for the various stages of brief writing will be provided. It will also discuss the differences and similarities between supreme court briefs and trial or intermediate appellate level persuasive writing.

A. FIRST THINGS FIRST: ASSESSING PREVIOUS EXPERIENCES AND SETTING GOALS

When beginning any new project, it is a good idea to start with an assessment of your current skills and experience. Thus, before drafting the competition brief, consider how your previous experiences will help you approach the competition problem. Use the "Assessing Previous Experiences and Setting Goals" questionnaire below to assess your current skills and experience in research, writing, and public speaking. Please note this is not limited to legal research, writing, or speaking. Indeed, you should consider all of your relevant experience to assess your current level of preparedness for drafting your team brief. Consider how that experience should be integrated into drafting the competition brief and your preparation and approach to oral argument. Each team member should complete the worksheet and then share it with their coaches and teammates. Use the answers for discussion and goal setting—i.e., what you hope to learn through participation in moot court.

ASSESSING PREVIOUS EXPERIENCES
AND SETTING GOALS

Writing in the space provided, please respond to each question.

1. Identify five characteristics of an appellate brief.

   _____

   _____

   _____

   _____

2. In light of your experience, identify one aspect of the researching and writing process that you plan to continue.

   _____

   _____

   _____

   _____

3. In light of your experience, identify one aspect of the researching and writing process that you plan to alter. Explain what alteration you would make and why.

   _____

   _____

   _____

   _____

4. What opportunities and challenges are presented in researching and writing an appellate brief?

   _____

   _____

   _____

   _____

5. How does (or could) the standard of review influence your approach to an appellate brief? How would it affect your approach to a supreme court brief?

   _____

   _____

   _____

   _____

6. How does (or could) a split among lower level appellate courts affect your approach to a supreme court brief?

_____

_____

_____

_____

7. In considering the approach to the research and writing process, does it make a difference which party you represent (Appellant v. Appellee or Petitioner v. Respondent)? If so, how would your approach differ? Why?

_____

_____

_____

_____

8. Supreme court briefs tend to rely on more policy-based arguments than you may have experienced in drafting briefs for class assignments. That is, those briefs look less at the instant case's facts and more at the broader policy implications of any legal decision reached by the court. With that in mind, review your answer to question 1 above. Which of the five characteristics of an intermediate appellate brief are similarly relevant to a supreme court brief? Why? Which are not? Why?

_____

_____

_____

_____

9. What individual strengths do you bring to the brief-writing process? What concerns do you have about your abilities?

_____

_____

_____

_____

WORKSHEET

B. COLLABORATIVE BRIEF-WRITING STRATEGIES AND TIPS

Collaborative writing is the process of two or more individuals working together to produce a single, cohesive, and complete document. Working with a teammate to draft the brief can bring challenges as well as benefits. The benefits include having a partner to explore research possibilities, to discuss the validity of proposed arguments, and to proofread. The challenges include depending on another person's schedule to complete a complex writing project while ensuring that all team members are included in the process and that all have a say in the words that end up in the brief. Ideally, the entire process, from initial read of the problem to the final submission of the brief, should be collaborative. Below, we will discuss strategies to help advocates best take advantage of the benefits while minimizing the challenges of collaborative writing.

To get into the mindset of collaborative writing, start with the use of collaborative language to describe the team's brief. This will establish right away that the brief is a group effort to be undertaken by all members of the team, locating responsibility with the team rather than any one member. Furthermore, the way we talk about things can have a prescriptive as well as a descriptive effect on our thinking. This means that we are often revealing how we think about the subject matter at hand by our very word choice. That is the descriptive component. However, we can also influence our own thinking by being intentional in our own word choice. In that way, the words we use can influence how we think. For instance, rather than using possessive pronouns such as "my," "you," "his," "her," or "their" when discussing your team's brief, use possessive pronouns such as "ours" and "we." Think of the brief writing not as something "I" am working on, but that something "we" are creating together. That switch in thinking alone can help you recognize that the brief is a team effort and that every team member's input is not only valued, but expected and necessary.

In coordination with student and/or faculty coaches, teammates should create a research and writing schedule to be respected by all. The goal should be to create a schedule that every team member and coach agrees with—and that every team member and coach can adhere to. While it may seem obvious, the point of drafting a schedule is not just jotting down a suggested timeline or putting down random deadlines. Instead, the schedule must be realistic about deadlines. In short, do not set impossible deadlines team members cannot meet. This requires that each team member be candid about their abilities to meet the deadline, given competing demands on their time, but also that they be candid about how their particular writing strengths and weaknesses may affect those deadlines. For instance, if you know you struggle with grammar rules but are a whiz at citation format, adjust the schedule so there is more time for proofreading and less time for the final citation check.

Coaches may be tempted to set a schedule that team members must adhere to. Doing so, however, may ultimately undermine the deadlines. Working collaboratively to agree to deadlines has the benefit of ensuring that everyone agrees and is equally obligated to a mutually set timetable. To further ensure compliance, consider having all involved sign a commitment to the schedule. This means that once the drafting schedule is completed, each team member signs an agreement to abide by the schedule. That formality may seem unnecessary amongst classmates, but it can also highlight the importance of meeting obligations. Meeting scheduled deadlines is essential not only to completing the brief in time for submission, but also for building team cooperation. When writing collaboratively, respecting the schedule demonstrates respect for your teammates' time.

That being said, each team member must remember that the competition sets the ultimate deadline and that deadline is not negotiable. Accordingly, team members should strive to be flexible and realistic about their availability. Drafting the schedule may require negotiation with coaches and teammates. In negotiating the schedule, respect your teammates' and coaches' time. That means respecting their competing obligations. Law students are notoriously busy and will have class, externship, work, and family obligations that will affect each student differently. Given the relatively short timeline for submitting a competition brief, competitors must recognize that they may have to prioritize time conflicts and even forgo some events to complete tasks on time. For instance, a shopping outing with friends is not a legitimate reason to miss a deadline, but a best friend's wedding may be. A mid-term examination is legitimate; an intramural basketball game is not.

While working within the schedule, establish a pattern of regular contact that fosters conversation. Circulate email updates every 48 to 72 hours with progress updates (e.g., tasks completed, tasks to be completed, and roadblocks hit). Schedule at least one thirty minute, in-person meeting each week. Because law students are busy—and moot court students busier still—prepare for these meetings by establishing an agenda so that the discussions are productive. For instance, no later than two hours before the meeting, provide a general structure of the meeting by identifying two to three points, tasks, or concerns to discuss. Be sure to leave the last five minutes of the meeting unstructured for anyone to raise points, tasks, or concerns. Setting aside that time for specific unstructured conversation can hopefully forestall the entire meeting becoming a gripe session. If logistics prevent in-person meetings, use Skype or other video-conferencing applications to ensure regular contact. Similarly, for drafting, you might use applications such as Google Docs or shared cloud servers that allow easy access to research and drafting files for all team members.

In all interactions, be respectful of the opinion of others. Remember, you are drafting as a team and every member of the team has an equal ownership interest in the outcome. Disagreement over legal arguments or strategy should not be made—or taken—personally. Rather, teammates will come to the competition with different expectations and biases that will color their impressions and opinions. But keep in mind that no student agrees to take on the work-load of moot court looking to do poorly or to undermine the team effort. Assume the best of intentions of your teammates.

In any collaborative project, there will be challenges and disagreements. This is especially true when stress is added to the mix, as it will be as deadlines loom. It might be tempting to ignore small disagreements to avoid awkward discussions. However, ignoring even small disagreements often allows them to fester. When the stress increases as the deadlines approach, those small conflicts can add up, leading to a more full-fledged conflict that disrupts the team and the drafting process. Defuse that possibility by addressing concerns candidly and early.

When discussing disagreements, there are several conflict resolution strategies you can employ. First, start by recognizing that all team members have a mutual objective—to complete and submit an excellent brief. Team members also want to be heard and have their ideas heard and their views respected. Second, separate the conflict from the people. The reason lawyers presenting arguments address the judge and the court rather than each other is because the issues being argued are not personal between the advocates. Indeed, our court system strives to separate the person from the legal issue precisely to avoid violent conflict by relying on professional advocates and rules of procedure rather than arguments between the directly affected parties. Model that behavior with your teammates. To prepare for that discussion, consider precisely what the conflict concerns. What is it that you are upset about? Isolate that issue from the person and avoid attributing negative motives or feelings to the other team member. Consider why the choice matters to you. What difference will it produce in the final brief? How will that affect the argument you are making? Third, in speaking about the conflict, use statements describing how you feel and why. That does not mean name-calling or haranguing; it means describing the specific problematic behavior and the specific consequences that behavior is producing to which you object. Propose a solution to resolve the current conflict and to present further conflict on that point.

If the team members cannot reach an agreement or consensus, take a break. The lapse of time may cause opinions to change. Another option is to seek other input. Consult a text or expert opinion (consistent with the competition rules) to consider a resolution. Indeed, before beginning drafting, team members should agree on which texts or experts will be consulted in the event of a conflict. For instance, select a grammar style and usage guide to settle disputes over language usage. Similarly, select a topical treatise or hornbook to settle concerns over the understanding of legal terminology. If the rules permit, designate one student to be "brief captain," with final decision-making authority over any disputes regarding language or legal arguments. Of course, assuming it is permitted by the competition rules, student or faculty coaches should always be consulted if the disagreements are more personal in nature or cannot be resolved using the techniques above. It is reasonable to feel frustrated. Indeed, one of the learning opportunities presented by moot court is learning to work cooperatively with your colleagues through disagreement and frustration. What counts is how you manage the situation to move past these obstacles, and that the team stays productive!

While you may be conducting research and writing independently, plan to work side-by-side through specific portions of the brief, specifically the following:

1. Initial outline development
2. Theme/theory of the case generation
3. Argument brainstorming
4. Question(s) Presented
5. Point headings
6. Statement of the Facts
7. Summary of the Argument
8. Final proofread/edit

Sample Schedule

Below is a sample schedule with deadlines for various states of brief writing. This schedule is for a competition that allows one month for drafting the competition brief. While competition schedules differ, this sample relies on a standard competition timeline that you can adapt for your own particular competition.

IMPORTANT DATES & DEADLINES FOR THE BRIEF

Day 1: Problem released, record reviewed

Day 4 (midnight): Question Presented due

Day 12 (midnight): Outline of brief, including identification of key facts, outline of the Summary of the Argument, and outline of argument sections

Day 20 (midnight): Draft of argument sections

Day 22 (midnight): Draft of fact and argument sections

Day 24 (midnight): Final draft (all parts)

Day 27 (5 p.m.): Final draft (all parts) with citations conformed to citation rules, formatted. Brief checklist completed.

Day 30 (5 p.m.): Final brief submitted to the Competition Committee and other school teams.

Note: Team members may submit drafts before the deadline, but they must be submitted by the date and time listed. The February 15 final deadline is non-negotiable as student coaches must have time to review and check for formatting issues.

ASSESSING COLLABORATIVE
BRIEF-WRITING EXPECTATIONS

After reading the material above, each team member should answer the following questions in the space provided; please respond to each question.

1. Do you have any experience with collaborative writing? If so, what worked well in the past to create a unified written document? What did not work as well?

   _____

   _____

   _____

   _____

   _____

   _____

2. What do you think would be an effective way to draft a brief as a team? Are there any challenges you anticipate in drafting a brief as a team? Identify any strategy you would employ to overcome such challenges.

   _____

   _____

   _____

   _____

   _____

   _____

3. Are there any additional challenges you had not contemplated before reading the material above? If so, identify them.

   _____

   _____

   _____

   _____

   _____

   _____

WORKSHEET

4. What resources or "experts" should the team rely on to settle conflicts or disagreements?

_____

_____

_____

_____

_____

_____

Once each team member has completed these questions, exchange your answers and then discuss your impressions and expectations of the drafting process. Be sure to include student or faculty coaches in these discussions.

C. HOW AND WHEN TO RE-ASSESS THE ACTION PLAN FOR BRIEF WRITING

The writing process is typically described as including five stages. Those stages are (1) prewriting, (2) writing, (3) revising, (4) editing, and (5) publishing/submission. Although these five stages suggest a linear process, writing is actually a recursive process. To move forward to the revising stage, the writer, for instance, sometimes needs to return to the prewriting stage.

Even though you developed an action plan, you will need to re-assess your approach to the brief and revisit your schedule throughout the brief-writing process. Some aspects of the research and writing process may take more or less time than expected. In addition, build in time to re-read the competition problem. For example, as you complete the research, re-evaluate the facts by re-reading the record. As you develop an initial draft of an argument, re-assess the brief-writing process by evaluating your initial outline. The questions in Section B of this chapter can be revisited as the brief begins to take shape.

RE-ASSESSING THE ACTION PLAN

Each team member should plan to complete the following additional prompts to help re-assess the action plan for brief writing during the brief-writing process. Review the brief and respond to the following prompts:

1. Focus on your identified strengths from the Assessing Previous Experiences worksheet. How does the draft reflect those individual strengths? To what extent does the draft not yet reflect those individual strengths?

   _____

   _____

   _____

   _____

2. On a scale of 1 to 5 (with 5 being the highest), how would you rate the persuasiveness of the text? Explain why you selected the number. In the explanation, identify at least five examples that are either persuasive or else present opportunities for increased persuasion.

   _____

   _____

   _____

   _____

3. Identify two aspects of the brief that need further development. Develop a task list of what needs to be done for this further development.

   _____

   _____

   _____

   _____

As with the initial assessment, each team member should exchange responses and discuss impressions. Include student or faculty coaches in these discussions.

D. RESEARCHING THE POSSIBILITIES

The research process for moot court competitions will in many respects resemble your research process for assignments in the required legal writing courses. The authorities cited in the appellate brief should showcase the depth of the writer's understanding of the law. The number of authorities cited and the range of authorities cited may, however, differ. Research can quickly become an overwhelming process. This section shares some strategies to help you research the possibilities to develop the best arguments.

The first step in the research process is to review the record. Consult Section B of Chapter 2 to help with the identification and formulation of issues. Because the record will feature a variety of materials, including references to legal authorities, incorporate those cited legal authorities into the research process. Plan to review the cited legal authorities and use those authorities to find other sources. For example, review citing references and any authorities cited within those authorities.

Although the record will be the starting point in the research process, reviewing those authorities will not be the only research required. Many moot court competition problems will be inspired by recent events. For that reason, research the topic in news articles, blog posts, and practitioner-focused trade magazines. Moot court competition problems may also be inspired by recent cases and statutes. If permitted by the competition rules, review posted briefs and listen to oral arguments in cases similar to the competition facts.[1]

Moreover, situate the legal issues by expanding the focus of the research. Review treatises and practice guides on the general topic to understand how the legal issues interact and connect to other areas of law. For example, the competition problem may be a student speech case involving a post on social media. In addition to research in the area of student speech, review general First Amendment sources. This will help identify distinctions the law makes relating to speakers, audiences, locations, and topics.

Research Tips:

➢ Read all legal authorities cited in the record.
➢ Validate (i.e., Keycite and Shepardize) all legal authorities cited in the record.

---

[1] Briefs and oral arguments are available on many court websites. For example, audio recordings of oral arguments before the U.S. Supreme Court are available at https://www.supremecourt.gov/oral_arguments/argument_audio.aspx and https://www.oyez.org.

➤ Research secondary materials for background understanding, related issues, and larger legal context.
➤ Research recent news articles and blog posts.
➤ Review posted appellate briefs and listen to oral arguments.

E. THEME/THEORY OF THE CASE GENERATION AND DEVELOPMENT

Appellate briefs are well-reasoned, well-supported legal texts. They contain detailed and nuanced arguments. To facilitate the reader's understanding of the arguments, develop a theory of the case that allows for the infusion of a compelling theme.

The theory of the case and the theme are often used interchangeably. The theory of the case and the theme often overlap and draw on related concepts, though each has a distinct purpose in the appellate brief. The "theory of the case" refers to the legal theory and relevant facts that support the conclusion asserted. The theory of the case should encompass all of the arguments that will be advanced in the appellate brief. For example, the theory of a case involving a student speech case may involve the school's authority to regulate speech that is vulgar, lewd, and offensive. The theory of the case will include the underlying legal principle that freedom of expression is not unlimited, and will reference the key facts, such as the identity of the speaker, the context in which the speech is shared, and the language used.

While "theme" will likewise reference the concept of the limits of freedom of expression, the theme is a broader view of the conclusion asserted. Essentially, the theme answers the question "so what?" What is the harm to be prevented? What is the wrong to be rectified? In the student speech example, the theme would draw on the need for schools to protect students from speech that they cannot understand. The need for this protection means regulation of the speech. Using the theme, advocates must generate and then develop an accurate, compelling, and persuasive reason as to why the case should be resolved in the client's favor. By developing a theory of the case and a theme, advocates help persuade the reader.

To begin to develop the theory of the case and the theme, complete the following sentence in 35 words or less.

This case is about _____

_____

_____

_____

When completing the sentence, do not restate the issue before the court. Instead, use this sentence to convey why the court should provide the relief requested. Focus on developing one memorable, legally accurate declarative statement that is favorable from your client's perspective.

In developing the theory of the case, avoid clichés and rhetorical questions. Clichés are overused metaphors, similes, or expressions that have lost the power to connect to the audience. Clichés seem forced and often fail to properly reflect the writer's intention. Rhetorical questions are questions asked to make a dramatic point, not to request an answer. Who doesn't like rhetorical questions? Most members of the audience. After all, the brief aims to answer the court's questions, not interject questions. The question format invites a contrarian response. Even if no snarky response is provided by the reader, the question format promotes reader disengagement.

To continue to develop the theory and begin to identify potential themes, respond to the following prompts.

- Identify at least ten key phrases from the applicable legal rules.
- Identify at least five key facts from your client's case.
- Describe how the resolution of this case impacts future cases.
- Describe how the resolution of this case can be beneficial to society in general.

Re-evaluate your completion of the sentence "This case is about . . ." Consider how you can incorporate the key phrases and key facts. Also consider how you can extend the perspective to reference future litigants and society in general.

As you move from generating ideas to developing a theory of the case, have each team member write three different potential theories of the case. Then test the theories by sharing with the entire team. Evaluate your teammates' reactions. Ask your teammates what word or phrase is most memorable—either in a good way or a bad way. You may find, for example, that the theory phrased in the negative doesn't connect with the audience in the same way that a theory phrased in the positive does. Likewise, you may find that a particular word or phrase leaves an overwhelming impression.

Persuasive text aims to motivate the reader to do something or refrain from doing something. Presenting a theory of the case and then weaving a theme consistent with the theory throughout the brief helps persuade the court of the conclusion you are asserting.

F. USING NARRATIVE TECHNIQUES IN THE STATEMENT OF THE FACTS AND BEYOND

It is often said that law does not function in a vacuum. This saying serves as a reminder that the law is created from facts and applied to facts. In the brief, the facts feature prominently in many of the components, such as the Summary of the Argument and the rule applications in the argument section. Yet the section that most readily comes to mind when considering the facts is the Statement of the Case. Although the Statement of the Case offers opportunities to use narrative techniques, each part of the appellate brief also offers opportunities to use narrative techniques. This section of the chapter shares suggestions to use narrative techniques that will work throughout the brief.

The Statement of the Case includes both a recitation of the Proceedings Below and the Statement of the Facts. The competition rules generally permit the writer to determine the order of the Statement of the Case (i.e., starting either with the Proceedings Below or the Statement of the Facts). But each component of the Statement of the Case should be developed with care.

The Proceedings Below summarizes how the case came before the current court, from the filing of the initial complaint to the filing of the notice of appeal. The Proceedings Below also includes a summary of the court actions relating to the filings, such as whether the court granted or denied the motion of summary judgment. Individual competition rules may require a summary of the reasoning underlying each decision made by the lower courts. In general, the writer has freedom to determine how much specificity to include in the Proceedings Below.

The Statement of the Facts summarizes the actions that created the dispute. The Statement of the Facts is often considered to be the client's story. The Statement of the Facts includes all legally relevant facts (i.e., those facts that are relevant to the applicable legal rules and policies). The Statement of the Facts also aims to put those legally relevant facts in context by highlighting selected background facts (i.e., those facts that situate the legally relevant facts in context). Extraneous facts—those facts that are neither legally relevant nor helpful in understanding the background—are removed. Yet dry statements will fail to maximize the persuasive opportunity afforded by the Statement of the Facts. Use narrative techniques to develop a story. The point of view, description of the parties, the level of detail given to certain events or circumstances, and sequencing are all critical to developing a strong, complete Statement of the Case.

Indeed, narrative techniques will facilitate the development of more than the Statement of the Facts. Narrative techniques inform the drafting of all of the sections of the brief, from Question Presented to Conclusion. This section focuses on the following elements of narrative storytelling: (1) character, (2) point of view, (3) setting, and (4) plot.

1. Character

A character is a person, entity, or even concept that is a participant in the story. Within any story, there may be main characters, minor characters, and supporting characters. Stories generally have at least two characters: a protagonist (i.e., the hero) and an antagonist (i.e., the villain). The audience should root for the protagonist's victory and the antagonist's defeat. To create a compelling protagonist, the character should be three-dimensional. These three dimensions typically include a physical description of the character's attributes, an emotional or mental description of the character, and a description of the character's actions (past, present, and future). In contrast, to create a reviled antagonist, a one-dimensional or two-dimensional superficial sketch should be drawn by the writer. The superficial sketch dehumanizes the antagonist and promotes the reader's identification with (and empathy for) the protagonist.

Creating a protagonist can be difficult when the character is not an individual. Endowing a governmental entity or corporation with human traits can be difficult. One approach is to use an individual to represent the interests of the governmental entity or corporation, as is used in the following excerpt from the Respondent's Brief in *Miranda v. Arizona*.

CHARACTER-DEVELOPMENT ASSESSMENT

Read the excerpt below and respond to the questions that follow the excerpt.

> A law-enforcement officer is not, of course, merely an investigator of crime. He is often charged with the responsibilities of maintaining public order and preventing offenses. In fulfilling these responsibilities, he must frequently act without delay. The picture may be one streaked with confusion and alarm; the need for action may preclude, at that point, a reflective resolution of ambiguities. If a policeman sees two men fighting with knives, his responsibility is to take them into custody, although subsequent investigation may reveal that one was acting purely in self-defense.[2]

1. Being as specific as possible, describe the character depicted in the text.

   _____

   _____

   _____

   _____

   _____

   _____

   _____

2. How do you feel about the character?

   _____

   _____

   _____

   _____

   _____

   _____

   _____

---

[2]Brief for Respondent (U.S.) at 21, *Miranda v. Arizona*, 384 U.S. 436 (1966), 1966 WL 87735.

3. Circle words or phrases that influence your thoughts and feelings about the character.

_____

_____

_____

_____

_____

_____

WORKSHEET

In the example text, the writer has used one member of a governmental entity to represent that governmental entity. With this technique, the law enforcement officer personalizes the governmental entity, even though no particular law enforcement officer is referenced. The writer describes the responsibilities of the officer, and thus the responsibilities of the governmental entity. Examples of what the officer sees and must do are used as a way to showcase the perspective of the law enforcement officer, and hence the perspective of the governmental entity.

To develop the characters in your competition brief, respond to the following prompts.

- Develop a list of ten words or phrases that describe your party.
- Develop a list of ten words or phrases that describe the opposing party.
- What are the key actions undertaken by your party?
- What are the key actions undertaken by the opposing party?

2. Point of View

Selecting a point of view helps convey the character's perspective. The four points of points of view are (1) first person, (2) third person, (3) objective, and (4) omniscient. Often the most persuasive points of view are first person and third person, which allow the reader to see the circumstances, actions, and events through the client's eyes. In the following example, the writer uses point of view to share Miranda's perspective with the reader in the Petitioner's Brief in *Miranda v. Arizona.*[3]

> When Miranda walked out of Interrogation Room 2 on March 13, 1963, his life for all practical purposes was over. Whatever happened later was inevitable; the die had been cast in that room at that time. There was no duress, no brutality. Yet when Miranda finished his conversation with Officers Cooley and Young, only the ceremonies of the law remained; in any realistic sense, his case was done.

Miranda is the first actor presented in the excerpt. He is identified by name. The bleakness of the phrasing (i.e., "the die had been cast in that room at that time") and the use of punctuation (the semi-colon and the commas) places the reader in Miranda's chair. Ending with "his case was done" evokes a sense of the door slamming behind Miranda as he exits.

---

[3] Brief for Petitioner (Miranda) at 10, *Miranda v. Arizona*, 384 U.S. 436, 383 U.S. 903 (1966), 1966 WL 100543.

To craft the Statement of the Facts from your client's point of view, consider the following prompts.

- What action, event, or circumstance is first presented?
- What is your client's involvement in that action, event, or circumstance?
- At what point in the Statement of the Facts is the other side presented?
- What is the last action, event, or circumstance presented?

3. Setting

Setting refers to the physical place in which the story occurs. Essentially, setting is the "dark and stormy night." The setting establishes the context for the actions. For example, this excerpt from the Petitioner's Brief in *New York Times Co. v. Sullivan* used setting to frame the conflict between the parties:

> The century-long struggle of the Negro people for complete emancipation and full citizenship has been met at each step by a distinct pattern of resistance, with only the weapons changing, from lynching, violence and intimidation, through restrictive covenants, Black Codes, and Jim Crow laws, to avoidance, "interposition," "nullification," tokenism and open contempt. . . . For almost a decade, to this very day, there has been "massive resistance" to this [*Brown v. Board of Education,* 347 U.S. 483] decision. The State of Alabama has been a leader of the resistance.[4]

The excerpt includes a reference to time with the "century-long struggle," and acknowledges the events that occurred therein. Concluding with "The State of Alabama has been a leader of the resistance" squarely places the case in its context by establishing the setting.

To establish the setting for your brief, write a 100-word description of the location and time of the story so that the reader can visualize the context. Review the description to isolate which words or phrases are repeated more than once. Those are key descriptions to include in the brief.

4. Plot

Plot refers to the sequencing of events in a narrative. When writing a brief, we can get stuck conceptualizing the story as a series of events

---

[4]Brief for Petitioners (Abernathy, Shuttlesworth, Seay, & Lowery) at 19—20, *New York Times Co. v. Sullivan*, 376 U.S. 967, 376 U.S. 254, 1963 WL 105893 (internal citations omitted).

that must be relayed in strict chronological fashion. The events need not be ordered from the event that occurred first to the event that occurred last. The events at the beginning of the story set the tone and mood. Consider beginning, for example, with the event that acted as a catalyst to the legal issue. The story may end not with the final act that created the dispute, but may end with the implications of the decision to the present parties, future parties, and even society. The following excerpt descriptively articulates the beginning of the action:

> The New York Times, perhaps the nation's most influential newspaper, stooped to circulate a paid advertisement to 650,000 readers—an advertisement which libeled respondent with violent, inflammatory, and devastating language.[5]

This beginning sets the tone of the story. The writer establishes the *New York Times* as an influential paper with a specific number of readers. The use of the word "stooped" signals to the reader that the paper is not the protagonist in the story. In fact, the paper is about to cause problems. The use of the dash emphasizes the characterization of the advertisement with its "violent, inflammatory, and devastating language."

Explore the possibilities of plot by completing the following prompts.

- Write three different ways to start your Statement of the Facts. Consider different events, different moments on the timeline of events, and different points of view.
- Write three different ways to end your Statement of the Facts. Consider different events, different moments on the timeline of events, and different points of view.

When incorporating narrative techniques, remember that lawyers can't knowingly misrepresent facts or the law.[6] Nonetheless, narrative techniques offer opportunities to allow the reader to see the story behind the legal issue.

G. CRAFTING SUBTLY PERSUASIVE QUESTIONS PRESENTED

At its most basic level, the Question Presented (also termed the Issue Statement) presents the reader with the question (or issue) presented

---

[5]Brief for Respondent (Sullivan) at 28, *New York Times Co. v. Sullivan*, 376 U.S. 967, 376 U.S. 254, 376 U.S. 803, 1963 WL 105892.
[6]MODEL R. PROF'L CONDUCT R. 3.3 Candor Toward the Tribunal.

(or stated) to the court. But this one sentence does more than accurately reflect the issue (or issues) on appeal. The Question Presented frames the issue in terms favorable to the client by incorporating a theme, fact, or policy consideration. This section will discuss the importance of crafting persuasive questions presented. Specifically, this section will provide guidance on the content of the Question Presented, the phrasing, and structural choices. This section will then pull together this guidance by using examples from the U.S. Supreme Court case of *Locke v. Davey*.

1. Content of Question Presented

The first step in drafting the Question Presented is to determine what content to include. In terms of content, the starting point is the issue described in the notice of appeal. This issue will guide your review of the record, formulation of research strategies, and review of located resources. As you review the competition materials, isolate information for the components of the Question Presented. Typically, the Question Presented has the following three components: (1) the law, (2) the legal principle, and (3) key facts. These three broad components provide some guidance, but the formulation of each Question Presented will need to determine how broadly or narrowly to describe the issue, how specifically or generally to describe the legal principle, how specifically or generally the facts should be identified, and how many facts should be included.

The nature of the issue, the standard of review, and the level of appellate brief will inform the decisions on what content to include, what content to exclude, what content to emphasize, and what content to de-emphasize. For example, appellate briefs to an intermediate court of appeals center on the individual parties while tethered to the standard of review. The following is one of the three questions presented in the Appellants' Brief in U.S. Court of Appeals for the First Circuit case, *The Bronx Household of Faith v. Bd. of Educ. of the City of New York*:

> Did the District Court err in sustaining plaintiffs' Free Exercise and Establishment Clause claims, where the Policy is designed to advance the Department's reasonable and legitimate Establishment Clause concerns while, at the same time, avoiding improper government entanglement in religious matters, and where plaintiffs may conduct their worship services at another location?[7]

---

[7] Appellants' Brief, 2012 WL 4194511 (C.A.2) (Appellate Brief) (third of three questions presented) (capitalization in original).

In contrast, the appellate briefs to a court of last resort will broaden the question beyond the parties. For instance, in the petition for certiorari for the case above, the questions presented were reformulated to the following:

> The following questions warrant review:
>
> 1. Whether a government policy expressly excluding "religious worship ser-vices" from a broadly open forum violates the Free Exercise Clause and Establishment Clause.
> 2. Whether a government policy expressly excluding "religious worship ser-vices" from a broadly open forum violates the Free Speech Clause.[8]

As with all forms of legal writing, the text needs to be designed with reference to the audience. So, keep in mind the audience of your appellate brief—whether intermediate court of appeals or court of last resort—as you draft your Question Presented.

2. Phrasing

Now that you've identified the potential content, the next step is to con-sider the phrasing of that content. Of course, the Question Presented needs to accurately reflect the issue. But as seen from the above descrip-tion of the content, there are many choices a writer makes in crafting a Question Presented. The same is true for phrasing. Words are selected based on accuracy and neutrality of position. For instance, when writing a Question Presented for an office memorandum, the writer strikes a neutral, objective tone that is appropriate for a predictive text. In contrast, when writing a Question Presented for an appellate brief, the writer will be attempting to formulate a persuasive question. Thus, while the writer still seeks to be accurate, the writer should select the phrasing that will lead the reader to reach the conclusion that the writer is seeking to advance. Like all persuasive legal writing, the challenge for the writer is to be persuasive and yet subtly so. The text should not be too emotional or too dogmatic, both of which can undermine the persuasive-ness of the text. As we'll discuss in Section K, the writer should consider the connotation, denotation, and vividness of the words.

---

[8]Petition for Certiorari, 2014 WL 4804413 (U.S.) (Appellate Petition, Motion and Filing).

3. Structural Choices

Once you have the content phrased in a persuasive manner, it is time to evaluate the order in which you will present the material. The two most commonly used constructions are (a) "under-does-when" and (b) "whether."

With the "under-does-when" structure, the Question Presented is broken into three components and plugged into a fixed phrase. In other words: "Under [general area of law], does [relevant legal principle] apply when [one to four facts are given]?" For example: "Under Iowa family law, is a premarital agreement enforceable when the agreement was signed 24 hours before the wedding, one party was not represented by legal counsel, and the terms provided for an unequal distribution of marital property rights upon dissolution proceeding?" This phrasing is often used in office memoranda and may allow the writer to present the issue as an objective issue.

With the "whether" structure, greater variety of the order is permitted. Although the "whether" construction seems to be a sentence fragment, the understood meaning is: "This issue is. . . ." For example: "Whether the First Amendment permits a school district to regulate a student T-shirt that bears the phrase 'Pull me a Pint' that interrupted classroom instruction."

Although often described as a question, the Question Presented may end in a period or a question mark. The appropriate punctuation mark is dependent upon the sentence construction. If the sentence is a question (like the "under-does-when" formulation), the sentence should end with a question mark. If the sentence is a declarative sentence (like the "whether" formulation), the sentence should end with a period.

As you will see, these two commonly used structures can inform the structural choices for the initial draft of the Question Presented. As the arguments are refined, the formulation will shift. And that shift may require using an alternate structure. Thus, stay open to re-drafting the Question Presented as your understanding of the legal issue and arguments develops.

4. Examples

Let's pull together these thoughts on the Question Presented by analyzing some examples. Consider the Question Presented from the U.S. Supreme Court case of *Locke v. Davey*.[9]

---

[9] 540 U.S. 712 (2004). Certiorari was granted on May 19, 2003 for 02-1315 *Locke v. Davey*, 299 F.3d 748 (9th Cir.). The docket is available at http://www.supremecourt.gov/qp/02-01315qp.pdf.

The Washington Constitution provides that no public money shall be appropriated or applied to religious instruction. Following this constitutional command, Washington does not grant college scholarships to otherwise eligible students who are pursuing a degree in theology. Does the Free Exercise Clause of the First Amendment require the state to fund religious instruction, if it provides college scholarships for secular instruction?

Now, if you were writing an office memorandum, you might formulate the Question Presented like the following:

Consistent with the federal constitution and state constitution, may a state statute provide that awards from a publicly-funded college scholarship program should be based on the student's domicile, high school grade point average, SAT score, financial resources, and declared college major?

This is an open-ended formulation of the issue that doesn't advocate a particular resolution. A number of specific facts are included, but are phrased in broad terms.

While this formulation would be appropriate for an office memorandum, which is a predictive text that does not suggest a favorable answer, it would not be appropriate for an appellate brief, which is a persuasive text. Let's consider how the writer would approach this question in a persuasive brief. Consider the Questions Presented below from the appellate briefs filed in *Locke v. Davey*. Can you identify the parties? What phrasing informed your answer?

I. Question Presented from the Petitioners' Brief[10]

The Washington Constitution provides that no public money shall be appropriated or applied to religious instruction. Following this constitutional command, Washington does not grant college scholarships to otherwise eligible students who are pursuing a degree in theology. Does the Free Exercise Clause of the First Amendment of the United States Constitution require the state to fund religious instruction, if it provides college scholarships for secular instruction?

II. Question Presented from the Respondent's Brief[11]

Where a State chooses to award scholarships based on neutral criteria to financially needy, academically gifted students, does the State violate the First and Fourteenth Amendments to the U.S. Constitution when it discriminatorily strips the scholarship from an otherwise eligible student for the sole reason that the student declares a major in theology taught from a religious perspective?

[10]Petitioners' Brief, 2003 WL 21715040 (Appellate Brief).
[11]Respondent's Brief, 2003 WL 22137308 (Appellate Brief).

From the reading of these two Questions Presented, you probably concluded that the Petitioners in Question Presented A are the State of Washington and the Washington State officials, and the Respondent in Question Presented B is the college student.

For the Question Presented in the Petitioners' Brief, the key provision of the Washington Constitution is provided to set the stage for the issue, and phrased as a "constitutional command." The issue is phrased as a requirement for the state "to fund religious instruction." The focus is kept on the state and the Constitution and whether the Constitution can "require" the state "to fund religious instruction." This phrasing slants the issue towards the state's arguments.

For the Question Presented in the Respondent's Brief, notice how the State is also an actor, but an actor that is "choosing" to pursue certain actions that affect an individual student. These actions are described in a manner that is negative. The state actor is "discriminatorily strip[ping] the scholarship" and "violat[ing]" the Constitution. The individual student is described as "otherwise eligible," with the eligibility requirements being "financially needy" and "academically gifted." Furthermore, the student is described as "declar[ing] a major in theology taught from a religious perspective." This phrasing slants the issue towards the student.

The danger of any text about crafting a Question Presented is to suggest that there is only one possible formulation. Below, consider the other options for formulating the Question Presented in *Locke v. Davey* that are drawn from the filed amicus briefs. As you review the following examples, consider to what extent these Questions Presented are similar to and different from the Questions Presented in the Petitioner's Brief and the Respondents' Brief. Consider, for instance, the structural choices made by the writers, the phrasing used, and the description of the facts.

Selection of Questions Presented from Amicus Briefs in Support of Petitioner

1. The question presented in this case is whether the United States Constitution *requires* a State to fund an individual's religious college education when the State funds secular college education.[12]
2. Whether Washington is required by the Free Exercise Clause to fund religious vocational training as part of a general scholarship program.[13]

---

[12] Brief for the National Education Association as Amicus Curiae Supporting Petitioners, 2003 WL 21697737 (U.S.) (Appellate Brief).

[13] Amicus Curiae Brief of National School Boards Association, Arizona School Boards Association, Michigan Association of School Boards, Minnesota School Boards Association, New York State School Boards Association, Pennsylvania School Boards Association, Utah School Boards Association, Virginia School Boards Association, American Association of School Administrators, Horace Mann League, and Public Education Network, in Support of Petitioners, 2003 WL 21697733 (U.S.) (Appellate Brief).

3. This case asks whether Washington violated the Free Exercise Clause of the First Amendment when it followed a state law forbidding the use of public funds for theology degrees, as applied to an applicant studying to become a Protestant minister.[14]

Section of Questions Presented from Amicus Briefs in Support of Respondents

1. Whether a State may deprive an otherwise eligible student of scholarship funds made available to high school graduates based on academic achievement, financial need, and enrollment at an accredited post-secondary school, solely because the student elects to major in theology taught from a religious perspective.[15]
2. Whether a state law that denies a state-funded scholarship to a student who is qualified for it by virtue of high school grades, family income, and attendance at an accredited college in the State—solely because the student decides to pursue a degree in theology—violates the student's constitutional rights.[16]
3. Whether the Free Exercise Clause prohibits the government from denying an otherwise-qualified individual equal access to taxpayer-funded benefits solely because he has chosen to use the benefits for goods or services that have a religious character.[17]
4. Whether a state policy stripping students of scholarship funds based upon an arbitrary and irrebuttable presumption, resulting in an arbitrary and capricious classification of citizens for the purpose of allocating a government benefit, and creating a civil disability penalizing only those students who wish to exercise their fundamental right to the Free Exercise of Religion, Free Speech, and Association for the purpose of discussion concerning religion conducted from a religious viewpoint deemed anathema by the State of Washington, violates the First Amendment of the United States Constitution as incorporated via the Fourteenth Amendment.[18]
5. Does a State violate the first and fourteenth amendments to the United States Constitution when it refuses to award a state-funded scholarship to

---

[14]Brief Amicus Curiae of the American Civil Liberties Union, American Civil Liberties Union of Washington, Americans United for Separation of Church and State, People for the American Way Foundation and Lambda Legal Defense and Education Fund, in Support of Petitioners, 2003 WL 21715031 (U.S.) (Appellate Brief).

[15]Brief for the United States as Amicus Curiae Supporting Respondent, 2003 WL 22087613 (U.S.) (Appellate Brief).

[16]Brief of the States of Texas, Mississippi, and Utah as Amicus Curiae in Support of Respondent, 2003 WL 22118862 (U.S.) (Appellate Brief).

[17]Brief Amicus Curiae for Religious Universities and Colleges, Specifically the Association of Southern Baptist Colleges and Schools, the Association of Christian Schools International, Azusa Pacific University, Brigham Young University, the Catholic University of America, Loma Linda University, and Pepperdine University in Support of Respondent, 2003 WL 22137319 (U.S.) (Appellate Brief).

[18]Brief for Amicus Curiae Teresa M. Becker in Support of Respondent, 2003 WL 22087612 (U.S.) (Appellate Brief).

an otherwise eligible student for the sole reason that the student intends to major in theology?[19]

6. Where a State chooses to award scholarships based on neutral criteria to financially needy, academically gifted students, does the State violate the First and Fourteenth Amendments to the U.S. Constitution when it discriminatorily strips the scholarship from an otherwise eligible student for the sole reason that the student declares a major in theology taught from a religious perspective?[20]

5. Takeaway Points

The Question Presented may only be one sentence in the brief. But the Question Presented is more than "just" one sentence. The Question Presented encapsulates your entire argument. For that reason, the Question Presented will be the most frequently edited sentence in the entire appellate brief. Consider the content, the phrasing, and structure as you craft a subtly persuasive (and yet accurate) formulation of the issue. And don't be afraid to revise, revise, and revise!

H. DEVELOPING WINNING POINT HEADINGS

Headings. You see them everywhere. Whether in an appellate brief, instruction manual, or recipe, headings divide the text into manageable chunks for the reader to navigate. But you aren't writing headings for the appellate brief. You are writing point headings. What is the difference, you ask? A lot.

Point headings are a series of one-sentence conclusory statements that correspond to each argument contained in the argument section of the brief. All of the point headings will be reproduced in the Table of Contents, one of the preliminary sections of the brief. This represents the first time that the reader will see an outline of the arguments, and presents one of the first opportunities for the writer to persuasively characterize the case.

Because headings are so important, this section will share strategies to help you develop winning point headings. Specifically, this section will help you (1) select the appropriate content, (2) evaluate the possible structures, (3) determine the suitable number, (4) craft persuasive phrases, and (5) implement effective formatting. This section will also include point heading examples from filed appellate court briefs.

---

[19] Brief of the State of Alabama as Amicus Curiae in Support of Respondent, 2003 WL 22176100 (U.S.) (Appellate Brief).
[20] Brief Amicus Curiae of the Landmark Legal Foundation in Support of Respondent, 2003 WL 22199299 (U.S.) (Appellate Brief).

1. Content

Essentially, a point heading asserts the conclusion that the court should reach, and provides a compelling justification for that conclusion that is grounded in the facts, rules, principles, and policy considerations. Point headings provide the answer(s) to the Question(s) Presented. Thus, look to the nature of your issue(s), the critical facts, governing rules, and applicable policy considerations to develop the focus of your point headings. But point headings don't supply just a yes or no response to the Question(s) Presented. They also include the reasoning. That gives you lots of options in crafting your point headings. To conceptualize the options, complete the following sentence.

This Court should [desired legal outcome] because [compelling justification].

Just be careful not to overload the point heading with too much content. Save the nuanced, complex arguments for the text itself. If you have three reasons why the court should reach the conclusion you are asserting, try to present a broad reference that would encompass all of them. Point headings allude to key points and save the nuances to be explored in greater depth in the text.

2. Structure

Point headings are presented in an outline format. That means that the point headings may consist of headings designated with roman numerals, commonly called main headings. (The main heading format is used in Example A below.) The main headings may be subdivided into what are called sub-headings. (The main heading with subheading format is used in Example B below.) Main headings are usually identified with roman numerals, and subheadings are usually identified with letters. If you are going to use subheadings, you need to include two or more per main heading. In other words, if you have a main heading and only one subheading underneath that main heading, your choices are to either add another subheading or to blend the main heading and subheading.

As you will see in the examples in this section, point headings may be structured based on different grounds, steps of the argument, or alternative arguments.

3. Number

The number of point headings will depend upon the nature of your issue(s) and the arguments you construct. A tip is to plan to have one point heading per dispositive issue. Because of the nature of moot court competition problems, you will have at least two main headings. But should you wish to subdivide the heading into subheadings, just be careful not to get carried away. Too many main headings (and likewise too many subheadings) will over-segment the text. Over-segmenting the text will obstruct its flow and momentum.

4. Phrasing

Each point heading, whether a main heading or subheading, should be a complete sentence. Sometimes writers will decide to use only a key word or sentence fragment as a point heading, as in Example C below. But while a key word or sentence fragment offers the benefit of brevity, it may appear to be incomplete. Aim to use complete sentences. A sentence may be as short as two words or as long as sixty words.

Your point headings will echo phrasing from other sections of your brief, such as the Question Presented, Summary of the Argument, and Umbrella. So what persuasive strategies you have used will inform what phrasing gets highlighted in the point headings. As discussed in Section K of this Chapter, consider connotation, denotation, imagery, and accuracy with phrasing. Avoid jargon and legalese. Read the point headings out loud to test the persuasiveness of the phrasing. Maximize the opportunity to reference and reinforce the theme you have developed in the brief.

5. Formatting

Point headings should be visually distinguished from the regular text. Spacing and typeface provide you lots of options. In general, point headings are indented, single spaced, and use a different typeface (for example, bold, caps, italics, or underline) than the text. By indenting the point headings on both the left and right side of the page, extra white space makes the text visually pop. But indents are not the only way to leverage use of white space; you may consider using 1.5 line spacing (rather than single spacing or double spacing). Standard typeface conventions are to use bold and all caps for main headings. Subheadings are underlined and in initial caps. But a modern understanding of typography would have us re-evaluate these standard conventions. For example, all caps can be difficult for the reader to absorb. And in the internet age, all caps has come to signify shouting in anger. So, LARGE and SMALL caps (as used in law review footnotes) may be selected. <u>Underlining</u> is more difficult for the eyes to absorb than *italics*. Consider how to leverage formatting to increase the appeal of the point headings. One word of caution: Be sure to consult the competition rules to determine what restrictions may be placed on formatting.

6. Examples

With so many ways to develop point headings, the options can be over-whelming. To help make the options more concrete, consider the point headings from *Overton v. Bazzetta*.[21] The issue there was whether a ban on visits of minors by the Michigan Department of Corrections (MDOC) violated the U.S. Constitution, specifically the First, Eighth, and Fourteenth Amendments. As you read the point headings, consider the strengths and weaknesses.

Example A: Point Headings from Petitioners' Brief[22]

I. Prisoners Have No Right to Non-Contact Visitation Protected by the First and Fourteenth Amendments.

II. MDOC's Non-Contact Prison Visitation Restrictions are Reasonably Related to the Legitimate Penological Interests of Institutional Security, Safety, and Elimination of Substance Abuse.

III. MDOC's Restrictions on Non-Contact Prison Visitation Do Not Constitute Cruel and Unusual Punishment in Violation of the Eighth Amendment.

These three point headings are strong assertions about the arguments. By deciding not to use subheadings, the Petitioners keep the reader focused on three main points. The Petitioners mimic the overall decision in the brief to maintain the focus on the reasonableness of the institutional policy. (Remember, the point headings will be presented on the Table of Contents.) Indeed, the second heading expands upon what that policy is intended to do. The prisoners are never demonized or humanized, which might detract from the persuasiveness of the arguments and indeed undermine the credibility of the arguments. The focus is simply on the needs of the institution.

The structure of each of the main headings is altered slightly, reminding you that you don't need to have same sentence construction in each point heading. For instance, the first heading simply references the First

---

[21]539 U.S. 126 (2003).
[22]Brief for Petitioners, *Overton v. Bazzetta*, 2003 WL 163866 (U.S.) (Appellate Brief).

and Fourteenth Amendments while the third heading incorporates the phrase "Cruel and Unusual Punishment," in addition to referencing the Eighth Amendment.

Example B: Point Headings from Respondents' Brief[23]

I. Prisoners Retain First and Fourteenth Amendment Rights to Association Entitling Them to Reasonable Non-Contact Visitation.

II. All the Challenged Visiting Regulations Infringe Respondents' Fundamental Rights While Failing the Reasonable Relationship Test of *Turner v. Safley.*

   A. The *Turner* Standard.

   B. Prohibiting Visits by Minor Family Members and Former Prisoners Infringes Fundamental Rights Without Sufficient Penological Justification.

   C. The Permanent Prohibition of All Visits by Family and Loved Ones as Punishment for Two Substance Abuse Misconducts Is an Infringement on the Fundamental Right of Intimate Association That Cannot Pass the *Turner* Test of Reasonableness.

III. The Permanent Prohibition of All Visits by Family and Loved Ones to Prisoners Who Incur Two Misconduct Citations for Substance Abuse Constitutes Cruel and Unusual Punishment.

The first main heading in the Respondents' Brief flips the argument as structured by the Petitioners' Brief. The Petitioners' Brief begins by asserting that prisoners' have no constitutionally protected right to non-contact visitation; the Respondents' Brief asserts that the prisoners retain specific constitutional rights. The Respondents, unlike the Petitioners, decided to divide the second main heading by using subheadings. The subheadings allow the writers to break down the argument into steps or key points. This structure also provides the Respondents with additional sentences to highlight facts, principles, and policies. For example, in the subheadings, the Respondents' re-characterize the institutional policy. Institutional jargon is avoided. Instead of using "Non-Contact Visitation" as in the Petitioners' point headings, the Respondents use "Visits by Minor Family Members and Former Prisoners" and "Permanent Prohibition." Although each main heading and subheading should have its own focus, repeating a key phrase can be powerful. The phrase "Permanent Prohibition" is powerfully repeated in two of the headings.

As mentioned throughout this book, the audience guides and informs the writer's decisions. This includes the choices made when constructing the point headings. The framing of point headings will depend upon the level of court. Consider the point headings from the *Overton v. Bazetta* case that were filed in the U.S. Court of Appeals for the Sixth Circuit.

---

[23]Brief for Respondents, *Overton v. Bazzetta*, 2003 WL 469673 (U.S.) (Appellate Brief).

As you read the point headings, consider to what extent these point headings are similar to and different from the point headings in the Petitioners' and Respondents' Briefs.

Example C: Point Headings from the Plaintiffs-Appellees' Brief[24]

I. Defendants Fail to Demonstrate Any Clear Error in the Trial Court's Finding of Facts.

II. Prisoners and Their Potential Visitors Retain a First Amendment Right to Intimate Association that Can Only Be Restricted Consistent with *Turner v. Safley*.

III. The Trial Court Deferred to Prison Officials by Applying the *Turner* Test.

IV. The District Court Properly Held that Defendants' Policy of Permanently Banning All Visitation for Prisoners With Two or More Substance Abuse Misconducts, As Applied, Violated the Eighth and Fourteenth Amendments to the United States Constitution.

V. The District Court Did Not Abuse Its Discretion in Allowing Witness Testimony to Authentic Summaries Prepared Pursuant to FRE 1006.

Example D: Point Headings from Defendants-Appellants' Brief[25]

I. Prisoners Do Not Have A Constitutionally Protected Right to Visitation.
   1. First and Fourteenth Amendments.
   2. Eighth and Fourteenth Amendments.

II. MDOC's Visitation Restrictions Are Necessary For Institutional Security.
   1. Governmental Interest At Issue.
   2. Alternatives to Visitation.
   3. Impact on Prison Administration.
   4. Not An Exaggerated Response.
   5. The District Court Denied Defendants A Fair Hearing Under the *Turner v. Safely* Test.

As would be expected, the point headings reference the actions of the district court. But the one-sentence main headings are still conclusory, persuasive statements.

Developing winning point headings is key to developing a winning brief. Point headings visually pop from the page and conceptually segment your arguments.

---

[24] Plaintiffs-Appellees Corrected Brief on Appeal, *Bazzeta v. McGinnis*, 2001 WL 34787106 (C.A.6 (Ky.)) (Appellate Brief).
[25] Brief of Defendants-Appellants, *Bazzetta v. McGinnis*, 2001 WL 34787105 (C.A.6 (Ky.)) (Appellate Brief).

I. SUMMARIZING THE ARGUMENT

The Summary of the Argument is just what you would expect: a summary of the arguments from the section of the brief titled "Arguments." In practice, the summary functions as a reminder about the content of the brief. The summary is often read, or more likely re-read, before any action is taken on the case. So, the summary may be the first section of the appellate brief read by the court, re-read before any judicial conferences about the case, and re-read again before oral argument.

Many court rules will define the Summary of the Argument as a concise statement as to the parties' arguments.[26] Some court rules will specifically restrict the length of the summary. In general, the summary should be between one and three pages in length. Few if any citations to authority are included in the summary.

The summary often begins with an overall conclusion. This overall conclusion is then followed by a succinct but persuasive statement of reasons that support the appropriateness of the asserted overall conclusion. The point headings typically provide a structure for the summary. But the summary is more than just cutting and pasting the point headings into one block of text. Instead, the point headings should be expanded upon. The one-sentence point heading becomes one paragraph of two to six sentences in the summary.

As the summary develops, keep it focused on the rule application. In other words, don't summarize the rules. Focus on the application of those rules to your case. For that reason, wait to write the summary until after the argument section is finalized.[27] Once the argument section is finalized, take a blank sheet of paper and write down the most important aspects of your argument.[28] This becomes the starting point for the initial draft of the summary.

The Summary of the Argument can be an overlooked section. The summary should showcase key themes, concepts, and facts that will be explored in depth in the argument. The summary packs a persuasive punch.

Tips for Writing a Persuasive Summary:

> ➤ Use paragraphing to increase readability.
> ➤ Limit citation to authorities.

---

[26] *E.g.,* FED. R. APP. P. 28(A)(5);PA. R. APP. P. 2118.

[27] For a selection of summaries of argument from U.S. Supreme Court briefs, see Judith D. Fisher, *Summing It Up with Panache: Framing a Brief Summary of Argument*, 48 J. MARSHALL L. REV. 991 (Summer 2015).

[28] Another option is to record yourself reciting the most important aspects of the arguments. A transcript of this recording then becomes the starting point for the initial draft of the summary.

> ➤ Focus on your facts, not the law in general.
> ➤ Expand the points, concepts, and facts identified in the point headings.

J. ORGANIZING FOR THE AUDIENCE (IRAC AND BEYOND)

One of the characteristics of legal writing is clear organization. Each form of legal document has an organizational structure informed by the document's audiences.

The audience has both expectations and needs that inform all manner of choices for the brief, including organizational structures. The audience of the moot court competition brief is the competition judge. That means a focus on the competition rules is important. But think more broadly about the audience. The audience for an appellate brief is comprised of legally trained readers—the court, court clerks, and opposing counsel. Judges at the competition will be legally trained—whether faculty member or practitioner. In terms of expectations, legal readers expect the use of the organizational paradigm commonly referred to as IRAC (i.e., Issue, Rule, Analysis, Conclusion).[29]

The IRAC structure is actually designed for persuasive writing. Following an articulation of the issue,[30] the writer begins with a clear statement of the governing rule(s). The writer then explores the meaning and reach of the rule thorough presentation of relevant authorities. Because the reader has reviewed the Statement of the Case, the reader will be reading the rule or rule explanation—whether consciously or not—with reference to the facts. Then, when the writer relates the rule to the facts in the rule application, the writer is merely confirming the initial impressions of the reader. Persuasion works best when the reader is always viewing the authorities in relation to the facts.

Although IRAC is always a good starting point in the organization, IRAC does not need to be strictly adhered to in all circumstances. For most argument sections, IRAC may not be the appropriate organizational approach. For example, issues of statutory construction often deviate from the IRAC structure. Cases of first impression that rely upon policy considerations may also deviate from the IRAC structure. Consider the

---

[29] IRAC has many variations. You may be familiar with CREAC, CRARC, TREAT, or another similar formulation. *See generally* Tracy Turner, *Finding Consensus in Legal Writing Discourse Regarding Organizational Structure: A Review and Analysis of the Use of IRAC and Its Progenies*, 9 LEGAL COMM. & RHETORIC: JALWD 351 (2012); Gerald Lebovits, *Cracking the Code to Writing Legal Arguments: From IRAC to CRARC to Combinations in Between*, 82 N.Y. ST. B.J. 64 (July/Aug. 2010).

[30] The Question Presented will express the overall legal issue.

nature of the legal issues, the authorities, the facts, and your arguments to determine how rigidly to adhere to the IRAC format.

In addition to sharing information, the organization should move the reader forward. Topic sentences, also called thesis sentences, convey the focus of the paragraph. The paragraphs need to be complete, cohesive, and unified. Transition words and phrases link the concepts together from paragraph to paragraph and from point to point.

How the text is displayed on the page will impact the power of the language. Lengthy paragraphs with extensive footnotes challenge the reader's ability to engage with the text. Since the goal of persuasive writing is to motivate the reader to do something or refrain from doing something, the reader must be able to easily access and absorb the text. Visual presentation includes use of different typefaces, but also use of white space, placement of headings, and paragraphing.

The visual presentation of the text matters. To see the impact of formatting, try the following exercise. Select one page of your argument section. Remove all headings and paragraph breaks. Use full justification so that the text lines up evenly on both the left-hand and right-hand margins. Now notice how difficult the exact same text is to read in this new format. A text must not only be substantively accurate, but also visually appealing.

White space can be used to emphasize arguments. For example, the margins create a frame of white space. The white space at the beginning of the paragraph fosters a sense of anticipation in the reader. The white space at the end of the paragraph allows the last sentence to linger in the reader's mind. The first line of the page and the last line of the page will benefit from the extra white space as the white space helps highlight those points. Maximize persuasive opportunities by leading and ending with a strong point on each page. Likewise, the white space between paragraphs gives the eye a break from the characters on the page. Vary the lengths of paragraphs. A series of equal length paragraphs looks visually bland and static on the page. Paragraphs of varying length add variety and a sense of movement on the page by altering the white space surrounding the paragraph. Make sure to showcase your persuasive phrasing by considering the placement of words on the page and the white space!

K. HARNESSING THE POWER OF LANGUAGE

An appellate brief should be persuasive. Persuasive writing aims to motivate the reader to do something or refrain from doing something. The language used impacts the persuasiveness of the text. Just how to construct a persuasive text can be challenging. As Chief Justice Rehnquist wrote, "brief writing can be called a combination of art and science."[31] This section shares strategies to harness the power of language, and then provides an example of the application of these strategies.

1. Strategies

➤ Watch pronouns. Pronouns are used extensively in speaking. But in persuasive writing, pronouns can be dangerous. Pronouns require the reader to substitute the pronoun for the appropriate proper noun. In making this switch, the reader must disengage from the text. If you do use a pronoun, be sure to use the appropriate pronoun. Avoid masculine generics and use the gender inclusive "he or she." (If using "they" to be gender inclusive, be sure to use plural throughout!) Also remember that an organization is a singular collection noun. In other words, a court, legislature, government agency, or corporation is an "it," not a "they."

➤ Use passive voice selectively. *The brief was written by Isabel.* This is an example of passive voice. The actor in the sentence, "Isabel," isn't grammatically the subject in the sentence. The object, "the brief," is instead the grammatical subject. Consider how the sentence reads in active voice: *Isabel wrote the brief.* Using active voice, the reader's attention is focused on Isabel as the person performing the action on the object. Active voice permits the creation of shorter sentences that are more direct. On occasion, the writer wants to lengthen the sentence and to be less direct. Passive voice allows the writer to focus the reader's attention to the object, not the subject in the sentence. The fact that the brief was written is more important for the writer's purpose than identifying Isabel as the person who wrote the brief. Passive voice allows the following construction: *The brief was written.* Consider another example of the active voice versus passive voice: *Jack killed John. John was killed.* The key is to use passive on occasion for emphasis, rather than using passive voice as a default construction.

➤ Minimize use of "there is," "it is," "this is," and "that is"[32] constructions. Use these constructions with care. Like passive voice, these constructions allow the writer to hide the actor of the sentence, which can be persuasive. But overuse of these constructions can

---

[31] Chief Justice William H. Rehnquist, *From Webster to Word-Processing: The Ascendance of the Appellate Brief*, 1 J. App. Prac. & Process 1, 4 (1999).
[32] Also minimize use of "there was," "there were," and "it was" constructions.

sap the power of the language. After all, sometimes "there's no there there."

➤ Use quotes sparingly for greater impact. Paraphrasing allows for the tailoring of language for the writer's purpose. Paraphrasing also helps with maintaining a consistent voice. Quotations can also be a distraction for the reader, so save the quotes for critical language.

➤ Avoid casual language while also avoiding legalese. The text of the appellate brief should assume a formal yet conversational tone. Watch for the use of slang, contractions, first person (I, we), and second person (you). Unless these appear in direct quotations, revise the text to avoid their use. Although the text of the appellate brief is formal, it shouldn't read like an excerpt from Blackstone's Commentaries. Be careful of jargon and lawyer-speak. This is not the time to use "said" as a pointing word. "Said" is used as a pointing word in the following sentence: "The student attended said school." Replace "said" with "the," "this," "that," "a," or "an" as appropriate. The example sentence thus becomes: "The student attended this school."

➤ Deliberate word choice is important. Each word should be selected with care. Consider these tips to promote deliberate word choice:

  ○ Minimize so-called elegant variation. Is it a car, an auto, an automobile, a horseless carriage? Deliberate word choice means being careful of word alterations that don't correspond with a meaning alteration. For the brief, watch switching litigation roles. Are you using "plaintiff" in one place and "appellant" in another? Does this refer to different parties or the same parties?

  ○ Use vivid word choice. Consider what images are conveyed by the word. Consider denotation and connotation of words. Denotation refers to the direct, or primary, meaning of a word. Connotation, in contrast, refers to the associated, or secondary, meaning of a word. Read the brief out loud. What words call to mind a particular image or reaction? For example, what are the differences between the words "child," "minor," and "juvenile"? What are the differences between "cut," "slashed," and "sliced"?

  ○ Avoid nominalization. Nominalization occurs when a part of speech, usually a verb, is converted into a noun. So instead of writing "The attorney made a recommendation that the client update the client's Will." The sentence becomes "The attorney recommended that the client update the client's Will."

  ○ Omit throat-clearing phrases like "One should note" and "Let it be emphasized."

○ Use adverbs selectively. Avoid over-reliance on adverbs to supplement the text. Rather than increasing the strength of the text, over-reliance on adverbs can bloat the text with unnecessary words. Packing a text with adverbs can distract the writer from selecting individually strong words and allow the writer to rely upon weak adverbs. Watch, in particular, use of the following:
- Actually
- Apparently
- Certainly
- Clearly
- Essentially
- Extremely
- Naturally
- Obviously
- Only
- Just
- Quite
- Simply
- Surely
- Truly
- Vehemently
- Very
- Undoubtedly

○ Locate phrasing like "relating to," "concerning," and "pertaining to." These phrases are often used to vaguely suggest some connection between ideas. Revise the sentence to make the connection direct and clear.

○ Streamline bulky phrases:
- at that point in time = when
- due to the fact that = because
- because of the fact that = because
- in order for = for
- in order to = to
- in the case of *Strome* = in *Strome*
- subsequent to = after
- with the exception = except
- despite the fact that = despite
- in some instances = sometimes
- in the majority of cases = usually
- during the time that = during/while
- at such time = when
- for the period of = for
- in the absence of = without
- places emphasis = emphasizes
- prior to = before

- whether or not = whether
- for the period of six months = for six months
- in a situation in which = when

2. Example

i. Revise the Text

Apply these strategies to the text below to revise the text. Eliminate unnecessary words. Replace weak constructions with stronger constructions. (Citations have been omitted for purposes of this exercise.)

It is not necessary for a school to wait for chaos to regulate student speech. In the case of *Tinker*, the Supreme Court of the United States of America reasoned that "undifferentiated fear or apprehension of disturbance is not enough to overcome the right to freedom of expression." Rather, for the school to regulate student expression, they must be able to show that regulation was related to "something more than a mere desire to avoid the discomfort and unpleasantness that always accompany an unpopular viewpoint." Restriction of student expression is, as a consequence, permissible where the record demonstrates facts which "might reasonably have led school authorities to forecast substantial disruption of or material interference with school activities." In *Tinker*, the Court places emphasis on the fact that the only suggestions of fear of disorder stemmed from the fact that a former student in one of the district's high schools had been killed in Vietnam. Some of the former student's friends were still in school when the armbands were worn, and the school felt that if a demonstration occurred, it would be hard to control. It is relevant to note that the Court held that this was not evidence that would have reasonably led school authorities to anticipate that the students' armbands would interfere with the work of the school.

ii. Potential Revisions

The example text above could be revised in a number of ways. Seeing the possibility of options afforded by writing can be overwhelming. Yet revising and editing are key components of the writing process. Potential revisions are identified in bold below:

A school need not wait for chaos to regulate student speech. In *Tinker*, the **U.S.** Supreme Court reasoned that "undifferentiated fear or apprehension of disturbance is not enough to overcome the right to freedom of expression." Rather, for the school to regulate student expression, **it** must be able to show that regulation **was not caused by** "a mere desire to avoid the discomfort and unpleasantness." **Regulation** of student expression is, as a consequence, permissible where the record demonstrates facts which "might reasonably have led school authorities to forecast substantial disruption of or material interference with school activities." In *Tinker*, the Court **emphasized** that the suggestions of fear of disorder stemmed from the **death of** a former student in Vietnam. Some of the former student's friends **attended the** school when the armbands were worn, and the school felt that if a demonstration occurred, **the demonstration** would be hard to control. **The** Court held that this **fear** was not evidence that would have reasonably led school authorities to anticipate that the students' armbands would interfere with the work of the school.

L. POLISHING A WINNING BRIEF

You're now in the final stages of submitting your brief. Your team has worked hard to research and draft your best arguments and you're nearly ready to file your brief. You will be tired and feeling the time crunch. Nonetheless, use the final revisions to polish your brief to be the best it can be, and all your hard work will shine through. Focus those revisions on proofreading, editing for consistency, and conforming the brief to the competition rules.[33]

1. Proofreading and Consistency

While "[a] foolish consistency is the hobgoblin of little minds,"[34] some consistency is essential in presenting a brief that is cohesive. Because parts of the brief will be written by different team members, it is important that the writers make sure there is a uniformity in the writing and terminology, so the reader is not distracted by differences in voice, tone, and word choice.

The time to create this uniformity is preferably in the initial drafting stages, but allow time to proofread for consistency. A list of consistent terminology should be created. For instance, the brief should refer to parties by consistent names (e.g., if using "employer," do not vary between "employer" and "supervisor"). It should also use consistent legal terms of art. Confirm that case names are either underlined or italicized—but not both! Determine how many spaces (one or two) follow a period.

---

[33] While this section talks about these steps as part of finalizing the brief, do not wait until the last minute to address proofreading and formatting. Rather, review the rules early in the drafting process, as you may need to ask clarifying questions of the competition organizers.

[34] RALPH WALDO EMERSON, SELF RELIANCE (1841).

Proofread the brief throughout and set aside a specific time for proofreading at the end of the process. In proofreading, do not simply rely on word-processing software grammar and spell-check tools. Those tools are limited, particularly when it comes to spelling of legal terms. Edit by hand. Print out the pages of the brief to read for spelling, punctuation, and other grammar and style errors. One way to make this easier is to read the sections—or even the pages—of the brief out of order, so that your brain focuses more on the words rather than the substance of the arguments or the accuracy of the facts. Use the table of contents of the style guide your team selected to help generate a checklist[35] to guide your proofreading.

Finally, read the brief to ensure that the theme or theory of your case is consistent throughout. As discussed in Section 3 of this chapter, having a consistent theme is one way to unify the separate arguments presented by the brief problem. Weaving that theme through the entire brief is an important persuasive device. Ideally, the arguments presented will reflect a similar theme or at the least variations of the same theme or theory. However, even if each argument may ultimately rely on a different theme, it is essential that the brief be read to ensure that the themes do not contradict or undermine each other. Similarly, be sure that the non-argument part of the brief—i.e., the Statement of the Facts—is consistent with and helps establish the theme or theory presented in the argument.

2. Formatting Tips

Formatting briefs according to competition rules might seem a mundane task. But it is also one of the areas of the brief-writing process where brief writers have the most control over point allocation. While we would like to assume that our logical prowess and persuasive skills always carry the day, in a moot court competition—as in life—formatting also counts. Indeed, moot court competitions factor in the brief's compliance with competition rules in calculating the team's score.

The easiest way to avoid losing unnecessary points is to conform your brief to the competition's formatting rules. This section will discuss some of the most common brief rules. It will also discuss the value of using checklists in brief preparation to ensure that your brief's formatting does not undermine your brief's quality.

Although the rules may appear nitpicky, they are often a matter of fairness. Typeface requirements, margin settings, and page limits or word counts all serve to ensure that both sides in a dispute have an

---

[35] For more on the use of checklists in legal writing, see Jennifer Murphy Romig, *Checklists for Powerful, Efficient Legal Writing*, 17 No. 4 GA Bar J. 50 (Dec. 2011).

equal opportunity to present their arguments by establishing the space parameters in which the arguments may be made. At best, a brief that does not conform to competition rules may be seen as sloppy, which undermines the writers' credibility. At worst, failing to conform to competition rules may be viewed as an attempt to circumvent the rules of fairness, further undermining the brief's credibility and calling the writers' professional ethics into question. Thus, competitors should endeavor to follow the letter and spirit of their competition's rules.

Before drafting your brief, do not simply assume that the competition brief should be formatted according to the rules of your legal writing class briefs, or local rules that applied to briefs you filed in court. Every court has its own formatting rules. The most obvious place to start is by reading your competition's specific rules.[36] Use those rules when creating your brief checklist (see below). Include time in the brief-drafting schedule to review and proofread the brief just for formatting compliance. Ideally, at least two days before submitting the brief, each team member should individually proofread the brief, apply a brief "checklist" that includes formatting criteria, and ensure the brief meets each criterion.

While the brief rules will differ from competition to competition, below are some general guidelines or tips for drafting and formatting your brief for maximum readability and point allocation.

First, make a citation "cheat sheet" for every citation, using whichever citation guide is dictated by the competition's rules. Do this for every type of citation used. For instance, journal articles, cases, statutes, and regulations. Or, preferably, create a separate document with every source listed by its proper citation format. Include the full citation format and all permissible short-citation formats. That document will be useful in creating the brief's table of authorities. Each team member should have a copy of the cheat sheet to ensure the team members are conforming to proper citation style while drafting. Furthermore, in drafting, use full citations throughout, as moving text can mean losing the citation to which an *"id."* citation refers. Then be sure to conform to the short citation forms at the end of the drafting process. However, do not wait until the final draft, as citations can affect total word counts. Rather, wait until the entire team is satisfied with the organization of the arguments and sentences to conform the final citations to the required format. Be sure to use pinpoint page references for every citation to legal authority or to the record.

Second, for headings generally, always insert a new page break before any heading that does not have at least two lines of text below it. Note that another subheading does not count as text for this rule. Thus, if you have a

---

[36] If your competition is arguing in the United States Supreme Court, consult Stephen M. Shapiro, et al., Supreme Court Practice (Bloomberg, 10th ed., 2013). The competition rules always prevail, but this guide can be very helpful.

heading followed by another subheading at the bottom of a page, insert a page break before the main heading so it all moves to the next page. Typically, headings are single-spaced even when the rest of the text uses double spacing. That allows the headings to stand out, increasing their usefulness to the reader. Be sure to consult the competition rules regarding the capitalization of headings. Competition rules may require that headings be in all capital letters, that they use regular sentence case, or that they use initial capitalization formats. For competitions that do not specify any requirements, you will need to decide how to format the headings. If permitted, review briefs submitted in prior competition years for the heading format used in the winning briefs. Furthermore, consider how the words will look on a printed page when read by the competition brief judge. Remember, in the internet age, all capitalization is often viewed as shouting. That does not necessarily mean stating a heading using all capital letters is unwise. It may be entirely appropriate given the particular legal issue.

Third, if the brief exceeds the word or page limit, do not use creative formatting to work around it. As noted above, those page or word limits are often considered a matter of fairness. Thus, even though it is possible to use formatting tricks to force the text into the prescribed limits, adhere to the spirit of the rules by editing the brief's text for concision. Doing so also has the advantage of permitting the brief to contain more "white space." As referenced above, white space presents persuasive opportunities. Thus, rather than try to use formatting to force as many words on the page as possible, edit for concision.

Start editing in the least critical parts of the brief. And edit at the sentence level. Editing at the sentence level means eliminating any unnecessary adjectives or adverbs, throat-clearing phrases, and nominalizations. In addition, review your brief for unnecessary quotations. Instead, paraphrase where appropriate as quotations tend to be lengthier. Finally, use appropriate abbreviations to refer to the parties. However, avoid using lengthy acronyms and instead use descriptive phrases (e.g., instead of referring to the "U.S. Fisheries Service" as the "USFS," use "Fisheries Service").

Fourth, because the Table of Contents and Table of Authorities are the first part of the brief, making sure these tables are correct and properly formatted helps establish the brief's credibility from the very beginning. Be sure to set aside ample time for their creation and proofing. It is tempting to use technology to avoid the manual creation of a table of contents or table of authorities. Resist that urge. Using special coding or macros to generate tables of content or tables of authority can create problems when exchanging documents between computers as part of the drafting process between team members. Moreover, computer-generated text may differ in its spacing or tabbing in the final document. Instead, use the citation "cheat sheet" to create the table of authorities.

Finally, briefs typically have different page formats for different parts. For instance, the cover page will have no page number, the preliminary pages (table of contents, table of authorities, etc.) will be Roman numbered (i., ii., iii.), and the rest of the brief will use Arabic numbers (1, 2, 3). Consult the competition rules for the pagination formatting requirements.

3. Using Checklists

In conforming your brief to the competition rules, it will be easy for the tiny details to get lost in the hustle of last-minute editing. One way to ensure that the final brief adheres to the competition rules is by using checklists. In *The Checklist Manifesto*,[37] the author notes that many mistakes are not a consequence of what we don't know, but of a failure to make proper use of what we do know. Checklists are written guides that assist experts in harnessing their knowledge, by walking them through the key steps in any complex procedure. Surgeons use checklists. Pilots and engineers do too. And so should brief writers![38]

Of course, formatting a brief is not nearly as complicated as surgery. But, like a sponge left in a patient, the little details of brief formatting are easy to miss. And these little mistakes can cost competitors valuable points. With that in mind, use the competition rules and any judging rubrics or evaluation criteria provided by the competition organizers to create a formatting checklist before you start writing your brief.[39] Two days before submitting the brief, each team member should separately apply the checklist and ensure the brief meets each criteria. The following worksheet lists suggestions for what a checklist should include.

---

[37] Atul Gawande, The Checklist Manifesto: How to Get Things Right (Picador, Reprint ed., 2011).
[38] Jennifer Murphy Romig, *Checklists for Powerful, Efficient Legal Writing*, 17 No. 4 GA Bar J. 50 (Dec. 2011).
[39] Drafting the checklist also provides an opportunity to review the rules for any questions or missing information. Then, if questions arise, you will have time to seek clarification from the competition organizers.

WHAT TO INCLUDE IN YOUR CHECKLIST

A. The checklist should include any requirements as to:

☐ Typeface (e.g., Times New Roman, Comic Sans)
☐ Type size (e.g., 12 point, 14 point)

Spacing

☐ Line spacing within a paragraph
☐ Spacing between paragraphs
☐ Spacing before/after headings
☐ Spacing between sentences
☐ Margins—top, bottom, left, right
☐ Page number requirements

Headings

☐ Capitalization system used (e.g., sentence case? title case?)

Note: If headings are to use title case, consult a style guide regarding the rules about which words in a title are capitalized and which are not.

☐ Typeface or type-size for headings (i.e., if the headings differ from the body text because of either the competition formatting requirements or the team's formatting decisions)

Cover Information

☐ Color of cover
☐ Case name
☐ Case number
☐ Court name
☐ Document name
☐ Parties' names
☐ Procedural posture
☐ Attorney/team name (or anonymous letter/number designation)
☐ Typeface
☐ Any lines or borders used?
☐ Binding of brief (if necessary)
☐ Required parts of the brief (list each part in your checklist with its corresponding format and substantive requirements)
☐ Order and locations of the various parts of the brief
☐ Format of Questions Presented
☐ Page limits
☐ Brief signed
☐ Certificate of service

Tables of Contents

☐ All sections of brief listed?
☐ Headings in Table of Contents match headings in body of brief?

Tables of Authorities

☐ Proper authorities listed?
☐ Authorities listed in proper order? (alphabetical, by court, etc.)
☐ Citations formatted correctly?
☐ Citations do not include pinpoint page references?

B. The checklist should include any other rules or information from the competition's rules not addressed above.

C. The checklist should always include the following steps, regardless of the competition's formatting requirements:

☐ Spell check?
☐ Grammar check?
☐ Manual proofread for errors MS Word can't catch?
☐ Block quotes formatted correctly?
☐ Every legal assertion cited to proper authority?
☐ Every factual assertion cited to record?
☐ Every citation conforms to Blue Book or other citation manual required by the competition rules?
☐ Every paragraph starts with a clear and compelling topic sentence that either (1) states a legal proposition or (2) states a conclusion on the facts
☐ The text of each paragraph supports the topic sentence
☐ Spacing between sentences is consistent
☐ Only one space between each word

D. Include other reminders important to your brief, which might include things like:

☐ Consistent theme between both arguments?
☐ Theme incorporated throughout all parts of the brief?
☐ Substantive points made from argument outline?
☐ Narrative arguments?
☐ Policy arguments? Policy solutions?
☐ Clear prayer for relief?
☐ Persuasive language?

WORKSHEET

CHAPTER 3
TIPS AND TAKEAWAYS

Although the learning process of moot court is not limited to the creation of the appellate brief, don't rush through the research and writing process in anticipation of oral argument. Developing a strong brief will provide a strong foundation to support the development of the oral argument.

- Budget time for prewriting, writing, revising, and editing the competition brief.

- Consider the audience and purpose as the brief develops.

- After each section of the brief is written, consider how the decisions in that section inform the other sections to ensure that the brief makes cohesive arguments and has a uniform voice.

- Create a checklist to confirm compliance with the competition rules.

- Don't forget to proofread!

CHAPTER 4
THE ORAL ARGUMENT

Congratulations! Your brief is written and filed with the competition organizers. Now is the time to turn to the heart of moot court, the oral argument.

A. LOGISTICS AND STRUCTURE OF ORAL ARGUMENT

Competitions may vary, but they typically follow a similar structure. In preparing for oral argument, advocates should familiarize themselves with the particular competition structure. Conduct practice rounds with that structure in mind so that it becomes familiar by the time of competition.

Before the arguments, there will be pre-argument logistics to settle. Advocates are assigned a particular courtroom, which may be a classroom, a meeting room, or an actual courtroom. Advocates should assemble in the room at least ten minutes before the argument round begins and before the judges enter the room. This is the time to settle your belongings, set out your materials, and take a deep breath.

Once the preliminary logistics are out of the way, the actual arguments begin. At the beginning of the argument round, the court will be called to order. This is usually done by a designated "clerk" or by the time-keeper. The same person will call the case, stating the party names, the docket number, and the name of the court sitting to hear the case.[1] When the judges enter the room, advocates should stand until the judges are seated and until told by the presiding judge that they may sit. The parties will then be asked if they are ready. Stand, respond "yes, your honor," and the first advocate for the appellant/petitioner should take her place at the podium.

As you get ready to approach the podium, remember to leave your pen and keys at the desk to avoid any temptation to fidget during the argument. And remember to button your suit coat and to take your hands out of your pockets. When you stand at the podium, it is acceptable to place your hands on the top of the podium, but avoid clutching the sides or leaning onto the podium. In small competition rooms, leaning forward can seem intimidating to the bench and clutching the podium can betray any nervousness you may feel to the bench. Knowing what to do with our hands when we speak is always a challenge, but use the practice rounds to develop habits that work for you.

Once at the podium, the advocate waits until recognized by the court before speaking. This means advocates must wait until all the judges look up from their materials and look in their direction. If there are multiple judges, wait until every judge is looking up before speaking.

When recognized by the bench, advocates begin the argument by addressing the court using an introductory phrase such as "May it please the court" or "Your honors." The opening is the time to introduce yourself, your co-counsel, and your client to the court. Typically, the first team member to argue will introduce herself and her teammate. The second advocate simply introduces himself to the court. The opening ends with a brief roadmap of the arguments that will be presented. For the advocate arguing first for a team, the roadmap should include a statement on the two issues that will be argued by both members of the team.

Typically, after introductions, the underlying facts of the case are explained to the court. Be aware that some courts do not want a recitation of the facts. This may be determined by the competition rules or by the culture of the competition. Thus, you should consult with your student or faculty coach for guidance on your particular competition. However, if there is no specific rule, assume the court wants you to recite the facts. That will give the judges the opportunity to hear your client's story, or else to ask you to simply dispense with the facts. If the judges do not wish to hear the facts, that means more time to argue, so just move on to the argument. For the advocate arguing second for either side, it is customary to

---

[1]For examples of the calling of a case, visit Oyez (oyez.com). Oyez maintains a collection of Supreme Court oral arguments reaching back to 1955, when the Court first allowed the recording of oral arguments.

dispense with the factual recitation. Nevertheless, you may wish to highlight one to three especially critical facts for your portion of the argument. Similarly, advocates arguing for the respondent or appellee have the option to develop their own facts, to correct any errors or misstatements by the opposing counsel, or to limit their recitation of the facts to filling in any necessary details omitted by the petitioner/ appellant. Keep in mind that the bench may begin to ask questions during the recitation of the facts. If that occurs, simply move into the main body of the argument.

The main body of the argument is where each advocate advances one to three legal arguments that support the team's theme. This is the part we most often envision when we think of oral argument. Indeed, it is here that advocates use the facts of their client's case to advocate for a particular result in the court. Unlike briefs, oral argument does not follow an IRAC or CREAC structure. Instead arguments are generally fact-driven—that is, arguments are focused on applying the relevant case law to the facts of the client's case. The main body of argument is also where advocates should expect to be asked questions and to provide thorough answers to the bench. In short, this is the point of the argument where the dialogue between the advocate and the bench takes place.

Each advocate's argument ends with a short closing. The closing tells the court in one sentence what it should decide and why your client should win. The closing should persuade the court to decide the case in favor of the specific relief requested. The argument ends with the advocate thanking the court and returning to her seat. Once the first team member has completed her argument, the second team member then approaches the podium. Once the appellant/petitioner arguments are complete, the appellee/respondent has an opportunity to present their arguments to the court.

After the main arguments are presented, the appellant/petitioner will typically have an opportunity to present a rebuttal argument. Depending on the competition, the appellee/respondent may then present a sur-rebuttal. There is no fixed limit for rebuttal that applies to all competitions. Generally, the amount of time permitted for rebuttal ranges from 30 seconds to 2 minutes. Because the appropriate time to reserve for rebuttal may vary by the legal issues presented, advocates should work with their coaches for specific advice. As a general guideline, advocates should avoid reserving lengthy rebuttal time. It is tempting to believe that more time will provide a greater opportunity to respond to opposing counsels' arguments. But judges often intervene in lengthier rebuttals by asking questions, which can prevent advocates from ending strong. Often a shorter time allows the closing advocate to deliver an uncluttered rebuttal that will be easy for the judges to remember and that will allow the advocate to end on a strong note.

B. ESTABLISHING AN ACTION PLAN FOR ORAL ARGUMENT

While the competition brief forms the backbone of preparing for oral argument, the argument itself will not simply be a recitation of the brief's arguments. Rather, you will need to adapt your arguments to a new and more diverse audience; the judges for the competition will include practicing attorneys, law faculty, and state or federal judges. Each judge's perception of the legal issues, and of your arguments, will be influenced by her experience and degree of knowledge of the subject area. This means you must prepare to argue before judges who will be thoroughly versed in the legal issues featured in the competition, as well as before judges who will have no familiarity with the issues—and to everyone in between. The keys to preparing to argue before such an uncertain audience include listening, being responsive, and staying flexible. Below are some guidelines to help you prepare.

1. Preparing Your Case

Similar to the page limits imposed by the competition rule, the competition rules will also outline time limits for oral argument. Oral arguments are limited to a set time for each side. That time is further divided between the advocates representing each team. Judges will ask questions during the argument, which will further limit the time for presenting discrete arguments. Indeed, questions from the bench will alter the course of oral argument as advocates focus more on addressing the judges' concerns than on a written text. Consequently, there will not be enough time to repeat all the arguments in the brief. Rather, consider oral arguments as the opportunity to demonstrate your mastery of the facts and the laws that most directly govern the competition problem and your client's case.

Oral argument time limits require that advocates pare down the brief arguments to fit within the specified limit. How best to do that may be determined by the competition rules, which may allocate equal time limits either per team or per advocate. For example, under the former approach, the rules may permit a team 60 minutes to argue, and allow the team to allocate that time however it desires between the two issues presented. Just as in allocating pages of the brief, in this scenario advocates should consider which of the two issues is more complex—and thus will require more time to fully educate the court about its legal ramifications—or is more compelling—and thus is more likely to persuade the court of the justness of your client's cause. In deviating from an equal division of time, keep in mind that moot court is a team endeavor, and an overly lopsided allocation of time could jeopardize the team's chances of success by not providing one member the opportunity to accumulate points. For instance, avoid allocating time so that one team member is granted 45 minutes, leaving the other only 15. Such a lopsided division may affect the judges' ability to score the advocates fairly—and may actually be proscribed by the rules, which may set a minimum time that both oralists must argue. Instead, start your practice rounds with the assumption that the argument time will be evenly divided. That will give each team member an equal time to practice. As you become more familiar with the oral arguments, shift minute by minute to find the right balance. In calculating this balance, be sure to account for any permitted rebuttal or sur-rebuttal time, which typically is deducted from the total team time allocation.

In contrast, competition rules may allocate the time per advocate. For example, a competition may dictate that each advocate should argue for 15 minutes. When the competition sets the time limit per advocate, the competition rules will specify whether rebuttal time may be deducted from the advocate who will present the rebuttal, equally from each advocate, or from either advocate as selected by the team. In the latter scenario, team members must again consider whether one issue is the more complex or persuasive. If so, then it may make sense to deduct rebuttal time from the less complex or compelling argument.

Regardless of the rules with respect to time allocation, every team must also decide the order in which to present its main two arguments. Barring a competition rule that states otherwise, a team is not necessarily bound by the order in which the arguments were presented in the submitted briefs. In some cases, the decision will be set by the legal issues involved. For instance, if one issue involves a threshold matter that must be decided first, that argument will necessarily be argued first. Similarly, if the issues involved are typically presented in a particular order in a majority of court cases, it may be prudent to follow that familiar pattern. If, however, that is not the case, the team will need to assess the relative strength of each argument and to what extent—if any—an understanding of one helps with an understanding of the other. For instance, if the two arguments are closely related and one argument provides background for the other, that argument should come first to assist the court. Otherwise, present your most persuasive argument first to start off with a strong first impression.

2. Preparing to Advocate

The first step in preparing for oral argument is preparing to advocate for the client's position. One impediment to client-based advocacy in moot court is that the client exists only on paper—in the advocates' imagination. Consequently, at least part of being an effective moot court advocate means finding ways to overcome the lack of a flesh-and-blood client. One way to do that is to create a biography for your client. Using the facts of the case from the competition record, construct a narrative. If the client is a human being, select a photograph for the client to help imagine her or his face. Use the record facts to get to know this "person," to construct motivations for their behaviors, to create someone to fight for. If the client is a corporation or government agency, research the business type or the agency to find out the type of work it does and how it helps its customers or constituents. Similarly, construct biographies for the opposition. Remember, moot court competitors argue both sides of any case in a competition. Thus, avoid creating caricatures or easy villains, as such characters will be difficult to represent. Similarly, avoid creating characters who are full of virtue and pure motives. Remember, no one is all good or all evil. Further, creating unbelievable caricatures may backfire by alienating judges who struggle to buy into the notion that the case involves a dispute between a clear villain and clear hero. Instead, try to create balanced characters to help you get into the role of an attorney and advocate.

As noted above, argument rounds are limited to set times for each side and/or each advocate. During argument rounds, there may be questions from the bench that will further limit the time to press any particular argument. Use these time limits to set parameters of what is possible to achieve in an oral argument round. Apart from team practices, practice your argument aloud on your own to develop a sense of how much you can say given the set time limit. For instance, if the competition provides for 20-minute arguments, practice your argument to ensure that it is less than 20 minutes to allow time for questions. Remember to think about your pacing as you speak; if you talk fast when you get nervous, practice taking deep breaths and slowing down. Record yourself and then listen to those recordings to ensure that your speaking pace is neither too fast nor too slow, and to account for any verbal habits (e.g., saying "um") that you will need to eliminate. Moreover, practice speaking in front of a mirror. This will help you become aware of any unconscious body or facial movements you may wish to alter or eliminate.[2] Similarly, record your private and team practice sessions. While few of us like watching ourselves on video, the video can help reveal unconscious nonverbal communication that may undermine the verbal message conveyed in the argument. Recording all practice sessions has the further advantage of creating visible proof of the progress you are making with each successive practice.

---

[2]For a discussion on the importance of nonverbal body language in oral argument, see Michael Higdon, *Oral Argument and Impression Management: Harnessing the Power of Nonverbal Persuasion for a Judicial Audience*, 57 U. Kan. L. Rev. 631 (2009).

3. Preparing to Open and to Close

All arguments begin with introductions of the attorneys and their clients. In your introduction, tell the court your client's name and her procedural designation. For example, "Your honors, may it please the court. My name is Stacey Smith and I, along with my co-counsel, Jeffrey Jones, represent the Petitioner, Iva Mae Brown."[3]

Next, introduce the case to the court. Do this by first reminding the court of the nature of your case and what issue the court is to decide. Do not state this in a neutral manner or simply restate the question(s) presented from your brief. Instead, this is the time to highlight your theme or theory of the case. For example, in a case involving the termination of a public employee, the advocate might introduce the case with: "The question here is whether a public employee has the right to speak on public matters without fear of losing her job simply because her boss disagrees with her opinions." Then ask the court for the specific relief your client seeks. "Brown respectfully asks this court to reverse the holding of the lower court and find that my client's First Amendment rights were violated." End the introductions with a brief overview of your argument by providing a roadmap of what you will argue. For the advocate arguing first for a team, the roadmap should include a statement on the two issues that will be argued by both members of the team. Then state the specific issues you will argue in one or two sentences, articulating them in way favorable to your side.

Plan your closing to be very brief—one to four sentences at most. By doing so, you can ensure that you have enough time to complete your closing. A short closing—under one minute—also prevents you from feeling compelled to start your closing too early, and thereby lose the opportunity to fully engage the judges with their questions. Ideally, you will be able to begin your closing with one minute left of your argument time. At the end of the argument, tell the court in one sentence what it should decide and why your client should win. Ask the court for the specific relief requested. E.g., "Accordingly, we/client asks that this court. . . ." End by thanking the court.[4]

Script your opening and closing.[5] Memorize them. Make both the opening and closing very brief so that you do not take time away from the substance of your arguments. Because the language will seem overly formal, practice speaking the introduction and closing until it becomes

---

[3] If arguing second as part of a team, simply introduce yourself to the court. There is no need to introduce your co-counsel again.

[4] Once the first team member has completed her argument, the second team member then approaches the podium. Again, remember to wait until you are acknowledged by the court before beginning your argument.

[5] For a discussion of drafting an opening statement, see Section A.

familiar and second nature. Practice your pacing as well as the substance of your opening to avoid speaking too quickly or too slowly. Practice alone to yourself, in front of a mirror, to your friends and family, in your car. The idea is to memorize the opening and closing so it is not necessary to look at your notes. This way your opening and closing will be poised and articulate. It also allows you to avoid looking at your notes, so you can make eye contact with the bench. While eye contact throughout your argument is helpful in persuasion, it is especially important in the beginning when you are making a first impression and at the end when you want to leave the judges with a final impression of confidence.

4. Preparing to Use the Facts

While some judges may ask that advocates dispense with the factual recitation, advocates should be prepared to present the client's facts to the court. In preparing to recite the facts of the case, do not simply list the pertinent facts. Rather, try to tell the court a story and organize the facts in such a way that they support your argument theme. If the bench wishes to hear the facts, do not rush through them in one or two sentences. Allocate approximately 10 to 15 percent of your oral argument time to your factual recitation. However, because the purpose of the oral argument is to argue, limit the factual recitation to those facts that are key to your client's desired outcome. Eliminate any unnecessary facts or extraneous details. For instance, include specific dates and times only when appropriate. But be candid. The goal is to present persuasive facts that do not allow the opposing counsel to object to any fact presented, or to suggest a factual misrepresentation in the subsequent argument or rebuttal. While you are typically not expected to cite to the record while reciting the facts, you should be prepared if asked to point out where your assertions are supported by the record. This will be especially true for references to key or highly contested facts.

The culture of competitions may vary regarding when and how often advocates should reference the record during oral argument. Regardless, advocates must be able to easily recall record citations when presenting their arguments. In representing clients, lawyers become familiar with the record because the facts of the case are discovered as part of their work as they interview their clients and witnesses, conduct discovery, and review evidence in preparation for trial. Lawyers, in essence, live the record's creation. Consequently, practicing lawyers are typically better able to recall the nuances and specifics essential to their client's case. In competitions, however, advocates receive a completely fictional record without having any prior association with the client or case.

Drafting the brief will provide some familiarity with the facts, as you will be citing and employing those facts in the written arguments.

However, it will likely not be enough to rely on the brief writing as sufficient preparation for effectively using the problem facts during oral argument. One reason is that, in writing the brief, you will write only one side of the argument. But in practice and in competition, you will argue both sides in multiple rounds. In preparing and presenting the opposing argument, you will likely find that facts that were not particularly useful in your briefs are nonetheless relevant to the opposing argument. Furthermore, you will find that during argument the factual bases of your arguments may shift, or you may be challenged by questions that bring to light the importance of an otherwise overlooked fact that was not necessary in drafting the brief, but is necessary to answer a judge's question. Consequently, you must use new tactics to incorporate the facts into your oral argument—tactics that help you select the most persuasive facts and that help you memorize the facts and record citations.

In reading the record, take notes on the most critical or "key" facts in the argument. Key facts include all the facts relied upon by the lower court in its ruling and all the facts relied on in the briefs of both parties. Ideally, your list of key facts should include any fact that, if it were changed or missing, would possibly call for an opposite conclusion. Once the list is compiled, generate a separate list of the most compelling facts for each argument. These will be the three to five most critical facts for your argument to prevail.[6] List those facts and be sure to integrate them into your argument. If your competition encourages factual recitation, use those facts to form the structure of your argument. If the competition routinely dispenses with the facts, or if the bench instructs you to do so during argument, be prepared to integrate those facts into your argument and into your question responses.

Ultimately, advocates must rely on memorization techniques to facilitate easy citation to the record in oral argument rounds and to effectively respond to questions. Keep in mind that judges often ask questions about the facts in the record—either because the judge wants to test an advocate's recall, because the judge did not read the full record before oral argument, or because the judge has been led astray by the opposing counsel's stretching of the facts! When judges rely entirely on the bench brief as preparation, advocates will need to be ready to fill in missing facts and to correct any misunderstanding of the facts for the judge.

To facilitate your ability to cite to the record, make lists of the key facts and the record page numbers on which they appear. Use those lists to make flashcards and use the flashcards to memorize the facts and the record citations. Another way to help memorize is role-playing. For instance, if the record contains transcripts, act out the roles of attorney

---

[6]Because you will argue both sides of the legal question, you will need to generate lists for both arguments.

and witness and read the transcripts aloud. Such role-playing can bring the facts to life, thereby improving memorization and enhancing the reality of the client you represent. Finally, consult the list of "missing facts" you have compiled throughout the competition brief-writing process and practice rounds. During oral argument, it will be helpful to know those facts that are not in the record to challenge an opposing party's argument or factual recitation. Keep in mind that it may be persuasive that some facts are missing from the record, especially facts that are essential for establishing the elements of a claim. For instance, in a case involving an age discrimination claim, it can be worth noting that the record contains no facts regarding the age of the employee hired to replace the terminated employee. To highlight that missing fact, the advocate would assert: "Your honors, the record contains no mention of the age of the employee hired by my client to replace the petitioner here."

Always remember that the bench may begin to ask questions during the factual recitation. When that happens, advocates need to be prepared to be responsive to the judge's prompting. Listen to the judge's question closely and answer the question asked. If the question concerns a simple factual clarification, it is acceptable to then resume the factual recitation after answering the question. If, however, the question is about a legal issue, it may be preferable to put aside the facts and simply move onto the legal argument, even if not specifically directed to by the judge. Remember, oral argument is a conversation. A judge asking you questions is indicating her areas of concerns. Thus, be prepared to depart from your outline to enter into that conversation with the court.

5. Preparing to Argue

Any action plan for oral argument should begin with a thorough review of the competition problem and brief. This review will be different from the one you undertook before writing the competition brief. Now your goal is to use the briefs as the starting point for your oral argument preparation. You will do that by reviewing the briefs and by considering additional arguments.

If the briefs of other competitors are available, those should be reviewed as well.[7] In rereading your team' briefs, make notes regarding the themes, the key facts in the case, and the key authorities relied upon. Read those authorities again. Read other teams' briefs and make similar notes; especially note any authority that was not used in your brief.

---

[7]Typically, competition organizers will post team briefs on the competition website. Be sure to check the website regularly for updates.

REVIEWING YOUR ARGUMENTS

After reviewing the briefs, answer the following questions:[8]

1. If the court can only hear one point in your client's favor, what should it be?

_____

_____

_____

_____

_____

_____

2. Where do you think the court is going to have the most trouble agreeing with your position?

_____

_____

_____

_____

_____

_____

3. Why should the court care about reaching the result you are advocating?

_____

_____

_____

_____

_____

_____

---

[8] Be sure to do this with respect to both sides of the argument, as you will be arguing for both parties during practice and competition rounds.

4. What does the other side have to prove in order to prevail?

_____

_____

_____

_____

_____

5. Consider the policy implications of your client's position: How would the result you are advocating impact society? What good would flow from a decision in your client's favor?

_____

_____

_____

_____

_____

6. Is the result you are advocating consistent with past decisions?

_____

_____

_____

_____

_____

While preparing to argue starts with the filed briefs, it does not end with those briefs. In preparing to argue, advocates in court can assume that the judges have read the parties' briefs—and consequently—that the judges will have some familiarity with the underlying arguments, authorities, and facts, and are ready to discuss the main points of controversy between the opposing parties. However, in moot court, it is likely that practice and competition judges will not have read the team's individual briefs.[9] Consequently, oral argument will depend on and yet depart from the written words of the team's competition brief.

Rather than view oral argument as an opportunity to read the brief aloud to the court, advocates should seize the opportunity to present their strongest arguments and to clarify any misconceptions or concerns the court may have regarding those arguments. Indeed, because your understanding of the arguments will continue to develop with each oral argument practice round, it is likely that the arguments made during oral arguments will differ from those in your brief. This is especially so when advocates argue off-brief.[10]

In preparing to argue, keep in mind that the points you need to make will not all be equally persuasive. Because arguments are timed, it is not possible to present every argument and counterargument to the court. Of course, the two main issues identified by the competition provide the first breakdown of the argument, and each member of the team will argue either of those two points. But within each of those arguments, advocates must further narrow the issues to focus on one to three critical points to argue in the limited oral argument timeframe. Consequently, order your arguments for persuasion and omit marginal arguments presented in the brief to focus on the arguments that are the most compelling or controversial for the court. The focus of your argument should be the one to three points that best support your theme.[11]

Use the answers to the questions above to organize the main body of the argument. For instance, the answer to the first question is the argument to present first to the court. Because the judges' attention will be most focused at the beginning of your argument, start with your strongest argument. This is the place to highlight the most compelling facts that support your argument, or to use the strongest case law that supports your legal contentions. Furthermore, because the court will probably interject with questions, it could be the only point discussed during the argument. Thus, be sure to select the most critical legal basis for your client prevailing as the first issue to argue.

---

[9] This is especially true in competition, where the team briefs are often scored by different judges than those evaluating oral competition.

[10] See Section C. Beyond the Brief: New Arguments and New Research, below, for a discussion of the differences between arguments presented in a filed brief and oral argument rounds.

[11] If none of the legal points support your theme, it may be a sign you need to change the theme!

The answer to the second question is the middle part of your argument. Because we—and "we" includes judges—tend to remember what we hear first and last, use the middle space to counteract some argument of the other side's, and also to clear up any confusion for the court. Sandwich the less persuasive argument in the middle of the overall argument structure. This means that if your argument is comprised of three points, your weakest argument should be the second point raised. Similarly, within each legal point, place the least persuasive argument within it in the middle, to minimize its importance to the bench. For instance, the middle of the argument is where advocates should explain away any unhelpful or contrary facts that may lead the court to reach the wrong conclusion. The middle of your argument is also the time to explain why a seemingly contradictory case or statute does not control the outcome of your client's case.

Finally, the answer to the third question will help select the final stage of your argument. Often, the last argument will depend on policy arguments or an emotional appeal that may help sway the judges to a particular legal conclusion. Because moot court advocates are expected to press a variety of arguments, it is useful to specifically set aside a time for policy-based arguments. Furthermore, while the tendency is to believe that logic and reason will always carry the legal argument, considerations of how a particular ruling will affect others who are similarly situated can often be what compels a court to act in a particular way. By appealing to the bench's emotions or pointing out the positive policy effects of a particular ruling, you end the argument by providing the court with a reason to rule in your client's favor. Leaving the judges with that policy proposal or emotional appeal can be an effective ending to an advocate's main argument. In competition, judges will score the round after arguments are concluded, so you want to leave them with a strong impression!

Practice rounds will assist you in honing in on the most persuasive or important arguments, exposing some unanticipated weaknesses and highlighting unforeseen strengths. Consequently, advocates should stay flexible about the arguments to be presented during oral arguments and about the priority of those arguments throughout the series of practice rounds. Revisit the questions above periodically to reassess the priority and organization of your argument.

6. Preparing to Answer Questions

As discussed in the introduction, oral argument is simply an informed conversation between an advocate and the court. In that vein, oral argument works best when it unfolds as a dialogue, not a monologue. While the idea of answering questions from a bench of three to four judges may seem daunting, welcome questions as a way to open dialogue with the court over the issues that concern the judges most.

For advocates, speaking for 15 to 30 minutes can be exhausting. For the bench, monologues provide no opportunity to address the concerns of the judges. While the prospect of facing a panel of judges all probing our understanding of a case's facts or law can seem daunting, the give and take of questions and answers is the reason oral argument exists. After all, if judges had no questions, they would simply decide the case on the written briefs. Thus, advocates should welcome questions as a respite from the sound of their own voices and as an opportunity to clarify any confusion for the judges, which gives advocates a chance to demonstrate their mastery of the facts and the law.

Part of preparing for questions is learning to recognize the various types of questions that may be posed. It is common to think of all questions as adversarial or hostile to our position. Those types of questions should be expected. Indeed, they should be welcomed as an opportunity to turn around a judge's thinking and to reveal the strength of your arguments. However, judges also ask questions simply to clarify their own understanding of a legal or factual point, even when they agree with an advocate's position. Advocates must listen for these "information seeking" questions. Similarly, judges often ask "friendly" questions. Friendly questions are typically designed to aid an advocate who is struggling, or to elicit a response that will be helpful to the judge when she attempts to persuade other judges on the panel to reach a particular decision. A common question like this is: "Tell us why your client should win." That prompt gives you the opportunity to launch into your strongest argument in response.

Preparing to respond to questions may appear difficult. After all, there are limits to what you will be able to anticipate. Nevertheless, from your work reviewing the competition facts, researching the law, and drafting the brief, you will likely have some idea of where the questions will arise. Indeed, most questions will spring from either the facts or the law implicated in a particular case. Thus, advocates should consider how the facts determine the outcome and, furthermore, how a change in any of the determinative facts would alter the outcome. Considering the facts beyond your immediate case can help you discern possible points of weakness as well as potential hypotheticals a judge may pose. Similarly, consider what rule you are asking the court to adopt and what effect that rule will have both on your client and on similar cases in the future. Consider why that rule is appropriate not only for your client's facts, but also from a larger policy perspective. What social good does it produce? What harms could flow from the court's adoption of such a rule?

Next, compare the appellant/petitioner briefs with the appellee/respondent briefs to identify the points of disagreement. If the parties are conflicted about a legal or factual point, it is likely that is where the focus of the court will be as well. Indeed, most questions will be about the areas of conflict between the parties, not the agreements. Thus, advocates must have a thorough understanding of the disagreements to anticipate potential questions. Likewise, much of questioning will focus on the counter-analysis of your own legal arguments. That is, advocates should expect to be asked about any facts or legal authorities that undermine their arguments. Answers will depend on the advocates' ability to explain to the bench why a particular fact does not alter the outcome, or why a precedent case does not control the resolution of the current dispute.

IDENTIFYING POINTS OF CONFLICT

To prepare to respond to questions, break down each argument and legal point and consider:

1. What are points of legal disagreement between briefs?

_____

_____

_____

_____

_____

2. Is there a conflict between the rules proposed by each side?

_____

_____

_____

_____

3. Is there a dispute over the implication of a particular fact or set of facts in the record?

_____

_____

_____

_____

4. How do the cases cited by opposing counsel undermine your argument?

_____

_____

_____

_____

_____

WORKSHEET

5. What factual differences exist between your case and the most compelling cases in support of your arguments?

_____

_____

_____

_____

_____

6. What is the primary reason the court would be reluctant to adopt your
conclusion?

_____

_____

_____

_____

_____

Looking for these conflicts can help identify the spots where the questions will arise. Use your list as part of your pre-argument brainstorming
to articulate possible questions from the court,[12] and prepare a response
to each question.

---

[12] This list will also produce arguments to be advanced when arguing the opposite side of the case.

7. Preparing to Concede

Part of oral argument questioning includes pressing advocates to the limits of the arguments being presented. Typically this is done with hypotheticals that stretch beyond the facts of the competition problem. The purpose is not to vex or frustrate the advocate or make the advocate look foolish, but rather to explore the realistic limits of any proposed conclusion. Remember that appellate and supreme court decisions result in rules that will be applicable to other cases aside from the one presented in the competition rules. While this is not strictly so, because a moot court competition decision is not binding on any subsequent cases, judges in moot court competitions have been trained to think like lawyers. And lawyers must always consider the implication of any proposed rule on the next case or set of cases that comes along. Consequently, moot court advocates must also think like lawyers and anticipate the possible implications of their arguments. For instance, in an argument about gun control, an advocate arguing against gun control would need to determine what limits, if any, she is willing to concede have some merit to avoid advocating for the right of every American to own a surface-to-air missile.

Because the court will try to press attorneys to the limits of their arguments, part of preparation should include considerations of when it is appropriate to make reasonable concessions. To prepare for concessions, advocates must consider the limits of every argument to be presented and which lines they are not prepared to cross for the sake of argument. This critical examination should be undertaken by both teammates together to prevent arguments or concessions that undermine or limit one another's arguments. Moot court is a team endeavor. Points are allocated based on both team members' performances. Be mindful, when considering and making concessions, that you do not concede the entirety or the foundation of your teammate's argument!

Practice rounds will help advocates explore these limits, because practice benchers will pose questions testing the argument or proposed rule. Nevertheless, advocates should consider the implications of their own arguments for future cases. This means advocates must be skeptical of the merits of their own case. Preparing to argue "off brief" will help with finding the possible points of concession, as you will be forced to look at the legal issues from both sides. Furthermore, as discussed below in Section C, part of the research process should include a review of literature from any advocacy organization addressing the legal issues implicated by the competition problem. A review of that literature can also help advocates identify the "parade of horribles" that will result if a particular decision is made by the court. Review those possibilities and determine their likelihood of occurrence, and whether their occurrence offsets the benefits of the proposed decision.

Concessions are hard. But they are often necessary to preserve an advocate's credibility. Avoid dismissing the question by simply stating that the hypothetical facts are not the ones before the court. As mentioned above, reviewing courts are focused on the next case as much as the current case. Instead, focus on explaining why the concession does not necessarily undermine the ultimate result the argument advocates. This does not mean to concede the entire argument or fold like a chair at the first sign of a pushback. Rather, avoid clinging to ridiculous positions or maintaining a rigid, inflexible rule regardless of the hypothetical facts pressed by the bench in a particular question. When pressed into a concession, do so gracefully. Keep in mind that even if a line of argument may create an untenable result under the question's hypothetical scenario, that does not mean the result is not appropriate given your client's—i.e., the competition's—facts. Accept the concession and move on with confidence that it does not alter the appropriate result given your client's facts.

8. Preparing to Rebut

It is tempting to assume that all advocates in a competition will make similar arguments, but that is not necessarily a safe assumption. Consequently, rebuttal can be difficult to prepare for because the goal is to respond to the arguments that are presented by opposing counsel in that argument round.[13] This means that while the appellant/petitioner is talking, team members must pay attention to the arguments being made so that they can effectively rebut those arguments. It is fine to prepare a bit of rebuttal in anticipation of possible arguments, but only by listening can you ensure that you will rebut what was said. Your team must be flexible and ready to listen to the argument while preparing an extemporaneous rebuttal. During arguments, team members may wish to share notes to prepare for rebuttal. Keep in mind that sharing notes can be a distraction to the bench. Thus, incorporate note sharing into practice rounds to ascertain your ability to do so as unobtrusively as possible.

Rebuttal is neither the time to make new arguments nor to reiterate the same points from your team's main argument. Neither should advocates "save" a point for rebuttal from their main argument. It is true that

---

[13] Because of the order of arguments, advocates for the appellee/respondent should recognize that their entire argument is effectively an opportunity to rebut the argument of the appellant/petitioner. Thus, many of the techniques discussed in this section may be applicable to the entirety of the appellee/respondent arguments.

the goal for rebuttal is to end on a strong note. However, do not sacrifice the main argument in the hopes of making a punchy point on rebuttal. One problem with such a tactic is that there may be a more compelling point to make on rebuttal, such as correcting a mistake the opposing counsel made or capitalizing on a concession. Another is that it can be viewed by the judges as sandbagging the opposition or, perhaps worse, can suggest the advocates were unable to prioritize their strongest points for the main body of their arguments. In short, saving the "mic drop" moment for rebuttal rarely works in practice. Instead, focus on any concessions or mistakes made by the opponent that influence the case. This is not the time to pick on minor misstatements, which could leave the court with an impression of pettiness. Rather, consider whether the misstatement affects the legal outcome of the case. If it does, use that opportunity for rebuttal. If it does not, or if there is no error by opposing counsel, use the rebuttal to clarify any points that may be troubling the judges. During the entire oral argument, advocates should pay attention to the questions the judges are asking to discern if there is one particular concern preoccupying the bench. Using rebuttal to respond to that concern—perhaps by providing an answer the opposing counsel could not—is an effective use of rebuttal time. Be careful in choosing to revisit a problematic response from the main argument, as doing so can unnecessarily highlight an error to the judges in the last moment of the competition. If the error is one that multiple judges appeared concerned by, it may be worthwhile to revisit the topic if it can be raised within the context of the rest of the rebuttal points—and if it can be resolved quickly. However, make the correction quickly and then move on to a stronger point before closing.

There is no fixed limit for rebuttal that applies to all competitions. Generally, the amount of time permitted for rebuttal ranges from 30 seconds to 2 minutes. Because the appropriate time to reserve for rebuttal may vary by the legal issues presented, advocates should work with their coaches for specific advice. As a general guideline, advocates should avoid reserving lengthy rebuttal time. It is tempting to believe that more time will provide a greater opportunity to respond to the opposing counsel's arguments. But judges often intervene in lengthier rebuttals by asking questions, which can take advocates off track from ending strong. Often, a shorter time allows the closing advocate to deliver an uncluttered rebuttal that will be easy for the judges to remember and that will allow the advocate to end on a strong note.

Given the short amount of rebuttal time, do not try to rebut every point made by the opposing counsel. Instead, limit your rebuttal to one or two points that go to the heart of your client's case. Rebuttal should be concise to have the greatest impact. After all, rebuttal is the last thing the judges will hear of the argument. Rebuttal should strive to leave a strong impression of your advocacy skills and your client's case. Once the rebuttal time is complete, thank the court and return to your seat.

Rebuttal time is reserved at the beginning of the appellee/respondent's primary argument, and the allocated time is deducted from the total time for the team's argument. In some competitions, the rebuttal time is taken from the team's total cumulative time; in others, it is taken from the advocate who will make the rebuttal; and in others, the team selects from which advocate's argument the time will be deducted from. Be sure to know your competition's rules and to consider the strategic possibilities of how to allocate that time.

The points made in rebuttal can be in response to either part of the appellee/respondent's argument. Consequently, to properly prepare for rebuttal, it is essential that both team members understand—and are able to articulate—all the arguments being presented during competitions. For instance, even if the advocate delivering the rebuttal argues the first issue, she must be prepared to rebut points made in the second issue argument if those are the most compelling, rebuttable points.

Some teams may prefer that a particular team member will always deliver the rebuttal. Other teams may prefer a more flexible approach, opting to select the advocate who will rebut during the competition depending on the selection of rebuttal points. Still other teams may switch who provides rebuttal depending upon which side of the case they are arguing in a particular round. For instance, one team member could be assigned to rebut when the team is 'on brief,' while the other delivers rebuttal when the team argues "off brief." Whichever approach your team decides, endeavor to work together during the competition to point out flaws in the other team's argument, and to select the strongest points for rebuttal.

Avoid the temptation to determine who will deliver the rebuttal at the last minute—i.e., during competition. In the stress of competition, emotions can run high. Leaving a decision on the rebuttal to be made within the thick of an argument round will only increase that stress. The advocate chosen to provide the rebuttal may feel she has inadequate time to prepare for that additional responsibility, while the advocate not chosen may feel slighted or undermined. It is best to avoid the potential for misunderstanding or hurt feelings by making the decision in the cold light of day—i.e., during practice rounds. Making the decision before practices begin has the further advantage of allowing team members to practice rebuttal during oral argument practice rounds.

If your competition allows sur-rebuttal, your choices of arguments are more limited. Typically, sur-rebuttal is limited to only responding to those arguments raised in rebuttal. Thus, it is even more critical that you pay attention to the arguments made in rebuttal. Just like with rebuttal, however, select how your team will allocate the responsibility to deliver sur-rebuttal.

9. Preparing to Use Cases

During argument, advocates will cite the legal authorities relied upon in pressing their arguments. You will have learned much about the legal arguments and the supporting cases during your drafting of the competition briefs. However, as discussed above, oral argument is not simply restating the same arguments contained in the brief. It may involve new arguments, as new cases may come to light during argument preparation.

In either event, advocates must be prepared to use the cases to support the arguments presented. Use the cases not just to articulate the law, but also to support the particular ruling being sought. In so doing, keep in mind that not all cases carry the same weight of authority. For instance, an intermediate court of appeals opinion is not binding in an argument to a supreme court. Similarly, a federal court decision will not carry the same weight as a state court decision when the matter before the court is one of state law. Thus, be mindful of the relative weight of authorities cited and prioritize the use of binding authority over persuasive.

The key in using cases is not simply reciting the facts or holdings of prior cases to demonstrate that you have memorized the cases' details. Rather, it is in applying those rules to your client's case to demonstrate how that case leads to a particular result. Just as you would do in a written brief, focus on telling the court why a particular case mandates a particular result, given the facts of the client's case. Do not assume that the law or facts speak for themselves. The court is neutral and is not looking for a way to support either advocate's position. The job of the lawyer is to advocate for the client's position.

A phenomenon unique to moot court is the expectation that advocates will provide citations throughout the argument. Typically, advocates will be expected to provide the following information during oral argument:

- Statutory authority: chapter, code name, and section;
- Precedent cases: complete case name, volume number, reporter name, pinpoint page reference, court, and year decided;
- Secondary authority: author, journal or publication name, year written, page number.

In some competitions, advocates are expected to provide a nearly complete citation every time a legal authority is referenced. In other competitions, advocates will only provide citations when questioned by the bench. Consult with your student or faculty coaches regarding your specific competition's expectations and history. Understanding the culture of your competition is key to understanding the competition's expectations for citation in oral argument.

Regardless of the competition expectations, moot court advocates will need to prepare to provide citations in response to questions.[14] Preparing to cite during argument is largely a matter of memorization. You've already completed many of the citations that were included in your brief. This is again a time to review that brief, making note of every authority used. Similarly, review the briefs of the opposition, noting the legal authorities cited there. For remembering cases, focus primarily on the main authorities. That is, the authorities that are most relevant to the client's case and that are binding on the court. Create flashcards or lists of the authorities and their citations. Review these cards regularly and update them as new authorities are added to your argument.

10. Preparing Logistics

Once the argument talking points are ready, prepare an outline and a few "cheat sheet" notes for use during initial argument practice rounds. Avoid using note cards, binders, or pads of paper. Note cards are too easily shuffled or disordered. Turning pages as required for a binder or pad of paper is distracting to the judges. Furthermore, it opens up the temptation to include too much information in the notes, so that an advocate is reading rather than presenting an argument to the court. Instead, use a plain file folder in which a few notes can be printed on the inside of the folder. You can either hand write the notes or tape or staple printed pages to the inside. Use an easy to read typeface in a font-size large enough to be readable while standing and without fully concentrating on the page (i.e., 14 point Times New Roman). The notes should include whatever each advocate feels they will need to remember. For instance, it might include the following reminders:

- Introduce self and co-counsel
- Introduce case/theme
- Key facts with record citations
- Roadmap/Argument points
- Conclusion
- Say thank you

The folder should also include "cheat sheets" to remember the details of the precedent cases and the record facts. For remembering the record, list the key facts and corresponding page numbers. Group like facts

---

[14] Citing to authorities or to the record during argument is largely an expectation of moot court competitions. In appellate practice, a judge may ask for a citation, but advocates are typically not expected to include the citation reference within their response as they are in moot court competitions.

together and use colored ink or highlighters to coordinate the facts to the legal issue they support. For remembering cases, primarily focus on the main cases relied on in your submitted brief and used by other competitors in their briefs. Include every case you intend to cite during the oral argument. Advocates will hope to talk primarily about the cases supporting their argument, but they must also be able to talk about opposing cases too—to distinguish the facts or otherwise explain what about that case does not control the outcome.

List the case name, the relevant citation information, and use a key word descriptor that helps you remember the case. Those key words might be either the facts or the holding of a particular case depending on what helps trigger the details of the case in the advocates' memory. Each advocate will have preferences for which details help her remember the case. For instance, for some advocates, knowing that a particular case involved a dispute over a barn will be more helpful than remembering the court's holding. On the other hand, for other advocates, knowing that the court held that the search was legal because a barn is not part of the "curtilage" will be more helpful. Include specific page numbers for facts and holdings so you can provide pinpoint citations when requested by the court.

As noted above, oral arguments often include questions from the bench. The number of questions—or whether there will be questions at all—tends to vary from bench to bench and round to round. Consequently, advocates must be prepared to argue either without any questions or with lots of questions. This means you will need two outlines.[15] One should be detailed, to explain more if the bench is not asking many questions. The other should be more focused on the main points that must be made, in case the bench has so many questions that there is little time for the advocate's arguments. During early practice arguments, take both outlines to the podium, but plan to quickly wean yourself from the use of any folders by the end of the practice rounds. Indeed, to avoid over-reliance on the folder, use at least half the practice rounds to argue without any folder or notes.

While preparing an outline for argument is an essential step in preparation, remember that oral argument is a dialogue between the advocate and the bench. That means advocates must be ready to alter their outlines to respond to questions raised by the bench. What you identify as the most compelling argument may not be the argument that most concerns the judges. Indeed, your arguments will be honed during oral argument practice rounds, and those arguments will only improve if you are flexible enough to stay within the conversation so as to answer the judge's concern. Thus, stay flexible when a judge takes you out of your prepared outline by raising questions about issues you planned to discuss later in

---

[15] Actually, because advocates will argue both sides of a competition problem, you will need to prepare two folders for each side. Be sure to clearly mark which is for which side!

your argument. Do not attempt to delay your response simply because you planned to discuss it later. Listen to the judge's concerns and respond to the question asked. Only after answering the judge's concern should you return to your argument outline. However, make sure you do not repeat a point you covered in your responses if your outline takes you back to something you already discussed.

Ideally, your folder should be nothing more than a tool to help you prepare for argument. It should not be used a crutch. This means you should not prepare the folder with an intention of reading from it during competition argument rounds. Rather, use it as a reference point to help trigger your memory or assist you with remembering details when asked for a specific citation. Thus, the text should be listings of words, not sentences. Almost every idea can be expressed in a countless number of ways to similar effect.

By the time you are ready to compete, advocates should be prepared to argue without any notes. Part of the advocate's role is to demonstrate that she understands the facts and the law and believes in the client's case. For this reason, you should strive to present your arguments without relying on any notes—or at most, on only the barest notes. Attempting to repeat a script word for word can undermine persuasion by suggesting that the advocate is simply reading, rather than presenting an argument she understands and believes. It can also reduce your speaking to a monotone or cause you to speak too quickly. Simply put, it is difficult to convey your belief in your client and the strength of your arguments if you must rely on notes to remember the facts and arguments supporting your client's case.

Furthermore, reading from your notes makes it easier to trip over words, as the focus is more on expressing the particular words in a specific order, rather than conveying the information to the bench. Reading also detracts from an advocate's ability to stay in the moment enough to effectively engage in a conversation with the bench. During arguments, your focus should be on the judges with whom you are engaged in conversation. You simply cannot engage in that conversation if you are watching words on a page rather than the reactions of the people to whom you are speaking. Looking at those words, you will lose the ability to assess the judges' reactions to your arguments and to notice the physical cues that signal that a judge is about to ask a question. Getting away from a scripted page is essential to fully engage the court in the dialogue that oral argument is meant to be. During argument you will need to respond to the explicit questions from the bench and to understand the bench's concerns that underlie those questions. Staying engaged in the conversation—rather than with words on a page—allows an advocate to really listen to the bench's questions, to get some sense of where the real concerns are, and to respond to questions before they are even asked. Finally, relying on notes means a lost opportunity to learn to think on your feet, which is one of the most important learning objectives of moot court.

While you should strive to avoid reading during competition arguments, a final—and separate—consideration is whether you should bring a folder to the podium during competition. For some advocates, the presence of any notes will be such a lure that they will not be able to avoid looking at the notes. Those students should argue without any notes to avoid that possible distraction. Still other advocates will find that they simply prefer to argue without any notes. The advantage of arguing without notes is that it can visually signal to the judges that you have mastered the material and that you believe in your client's cause. Keep in mind, however, that some judges may conclude that an advocate arguing without notes is too confident or is insufficiently serious about the competition. While this thinking is somewhat counterintuitive, it is important to be aware of your competition's culture. If your competition judges frown when there are arguments sans notes, prepare a folder to use as nothing more than a prop. Indeed, even if you intend to use a folder in your argument, you should consider it a prop, not a crutch.

The above steps are designed to help you formulate an action plan for oral argument. However, be aware that one of the most important skills to bring—or develop—in moot court competitions is the ability to reassess on the fly and adjust as needed. The view you have of the competition at the beginning of practice rounds will necessarily shift as you complete each practice round. Indeed, if your view does not shift, you should question whether you are paying sufficient attention and learning all that you can. You may find that one of your teammates has a more natural ability to provide a strong, pithy rebuttal. You may find that one argument is more complicated or more persuasive than initially considered, requiring a reordering of your primary argument points. Indeed, you may even find that by the end of practice rounds you have abandoned your initial three critical points in favor of three new points that are even stronger. Similarly, you may conclude that one of the legal issues is more compelling—or more complicated—and thus, that it should be allocated more argument time (if permitted by the rules). Consequently, be prepared to alter your action plan to meet the new understandings of the problem, the strength of the arguments, and the individual strengths of your teammates. The important thing is to stay flexible, with the goal of succeeding as a team.

C. BEYOND THE BRIEF: NEW ARGUMENTS AND NEW RESEARCH

The filed competition brief is the natural starting point for your oral argument preparation. Nonetheless, the competition brief should not be viewed as the end of your research or arguments. Rather, advocates should be prepared to continue their research throughout the argument process even though the briefs are finished. This will be necessary to prepare to argue the opposing side, to respond to questions, and to most effectively advocate on behalf of the client.

Once in competition, advocates argue both sides of the legal issue. Thus, while you may have written a brief for the appellee/respondent, in competition you will argue for both the appellant/petitioner and the appellee/respondent. Consequently, advocates will need to conduct research on the opposing side. Start by re-reading all the cases, statutes, and regulations relied upon in the submitted brief arguments. While the brief written by the opposition maintains an opposing view, read their authorities with an eye towards how they may be used to reach the opposite result. Look for any contrary citations within those sources that might lead to the authorities supporting a contrary result. In addition, conduct research to support the alternative view. If you've maintained a thorough research log, review any cases you discarded as unhelpful to your brief's cause—you may find those cases suddenly very helpful now that you are on the other side.

In writing the competition briefs, advocates have the advantage of controlling the flow of the written monologue. There is no give-and-take in a written brief. In contrast, oral argument is a dialogue between an advocate and the judges. And like most conversations, this one can become somewhat freewheeling, encompassing issues beyond those contained in the written briefs. Indeed, while competition judges will have some inkling of the legal issues to be argued, they likely will not know the specific arguments made in your team's particular brief. That is all for the better! Understanding the limitation of the judge's familiarity with your team's brief frees you up to go beyond the arguments in the brief— either into new arguments or to more refined arguments, as oral argument practices help hone your understanding of the legal issues. Thus, in anticipation of oral argument, your research should stretch beyond the limits of your written arguments.

Another consequence of the dialogue aspect of oral argument is that advocates cannot control what questions a judge might ask—or whether those questions stay within the confines of the legal issues before the court. This means that advocates must be familiar with the nuances of their own arguments. It also means that preparing to answer the judges' questions in oral argument necessitates additional research beyond the legal issues presented in the competition briefs.[16] Specifically, this means

---

[16] Of course, if you are asked a question that is too far afield, it is appropriate to respond that the question is one that is not currently before the court. That tactic, however, should not be overly relied upon. As unfair as it may seem, a judge asking a question expects an answer, and a refusal to answer—or a suggestion that the question is not relevant—may negatively affect your score. After answering the question, the advocate can then explain why that issue is not relevant to the legal issue before the court.

that advocates should consider those issues that may tangentially relate to the particular legal issue. To prepare to answer a judge's questions, go back to the list of facts and legal issues generated in the first read of the competition problem.[17] Focus on any extraneous issues you spotted that were not ultimately the legal issues before the court. That list may now be useful in identifying the issues a legal mind might consider when hearing the facts of the case or the legal arguments. Furthermore, review treatises and practice guides on your specific issue. In this review, consider material mentioned before and after the entry on your legal issue in these texts. Look for any footnotes or cross-references that may direct to topics typically considered related to your legal issue. If the legal issue involves a statute, step back from the particular code section involved and locate the code within the larger chapter or volume. A review of code sections before or after the one that is at issue may identify related issues.

Finally, additional guidance on questions beyond the scope of the legal questions will come through oral argument practice rounds. Keep a list of questions asked during practice. And take notes on the responses provided and whether those responses satisfied the bench. If what seems like a tangential question is asked more than once in the practice rounds, there either may be some confusion about the legal issue under discussion, or else that question is likely to be raised in competition. This information should be used to further develop the argument to avoid the confusion and to prepare answers to what may be inevitable questions.

As noted above, each judge's individual familiarity with the legal issues being argued will vary. Thus, in presenting arguments, it is advisable that advocates are able to minimize legal jargon and to explain legal issues using plain language to facilitate understanding regardless of the judge's individual expertise. To help accomplish this, research your legal issue within nonspecialized newspaper or magazine articles. Typically designed for a diverse audience, these articles are written for readers with no legal education, and rely on plain language to convey complex legal issues. Consequently, these articles may help you develop the ability to describe your legal position with the least amount of unnecessary jargon.

Similarly, include state bar journals and specialized legal newspapers in your pre-argument research. Bar journals are written for practicing attorneys, and will consequently use more legal jargon than newspapers or magazines for the general public. Nevertheless, these articles are typically written for a general legal audience rather than specialists within

---

[17] See discussion *supra*, Chapter 2, Section A.

the profession. Consequently, such articles will present the issues in language familiar to lawyers but understandable to a nonspecialized audience. Furthermore, these publications may include editorials or opinion pieces articulating policy or legal concerns raised by the legal issue or arguments in the competition problem. Such opinion pieces can highlight potential pitfalls or benefits to your legal or policy arguments—or those made by the opposing counsel. However, keep in mind that these sources are not citable as legal authority, and the descriptions of the legal issues may gloss over critical legal distinctions or avoid more complex reasoning, especially in lay-audience newspaper and magazine articles. Thus, advocates should use these articles only as a guide to incorporating plain language into their arguments.

Finally, oral argument is primarily about advocacy and persuasion. Advocacy requires passion and belief in your client's cause. To become familiar with advocacy writing on your legal issue, visit the websites of nonprofit or public interest organizations involved in issues implicated by your legal issue. For instance, if the competition problem involves gun rights or gun control, read literature from the National Rifle Association as well as from the Brady Campaign to Prevent Gun Violence. Search for blogs and podcasts that address the same legal issue. While none of these materials constitute legal authority, they can be invaluable in giving you the perspective of an advocate on your legal issue. In doing so, they may help you better intuit the direction of a judge's questions—or help you understand a particular judge's seeming hostility or enthusiasm towards your arguments. Advocacy materials can also expose the mainstream—and even extremist—arguments that drive public debates over law and policy concerning the legal issues implicated in the competition problem. Advocates should, of course, refrain from hyperbole during oral argument. Nonetheless, understanding these arguments can aid the development of your persuasive persona.

D. STRUCTURING PRODUCTIVE ORAL ARGUMENT PRACTICES

Once the briefs are filed, the team's practice oral arguments begin. For many competitions, practice rounds are the only mechanism through which student advocates may receive feedback from law faculty, practicing attorneys, or their fellow students. Below are suggestions to help your team make the most of this opportunity.

1. Scheduling

The first step to successful team practices is scheduling the practice rounds.[18] Start planning early. It can be challenging to find times when all team members, student coaches, and faculty coaches can meet. It can be even more challenging to find a time when that will coincide with the availability of volunteer practice-round judges. Practicing attorneys will likely be available in the evening, while law faculty will often be unavailable by that time. Consequently, try to schedule practice rounds both during and after the school day.

In scheduling practice rounds, also consider the form the practice will take. Typically, practices include the advocates, coaches, and two to three judges for a panel. However, the team may wish to hold "round-table" discussions, where the team members present their arguments and answer each other's questions. This can be done while informally seated at a table. While advocates should avoid informality when in competition, the opportunity to discuss the legal issues in this context makes it easier to conceptualize the oral argument as a conversation rather than a speech. Regardless of the format of actual practice rounds, be sure to schedule times for regular team meetings.[19]

The number of practice rounds will depend on the number of weeks the team has to practice. The more weeks the team has to practice, the more it can afford to have fewer practices each week. Conversely, the fewer weeks there are to practice, the more practices the team will need to fit into each week. While the impulse may be to have as many practice rounds as there are days in the week, avoid overly-rigorous schedules. Practicing too much can result in exhaustion, as well as a robotic, overly-rehearsed performance by the time of competition. Furthermore, too-frequent practices may undermine student advocates' ability to prepare for and participate in their other law school classes. It is ideal to have at least one day between each practice round to allow the team to process feedback and conduct any additional research necessitated by the team's evolving understanding of the legal issues based on that feedback. One approach is to start with fewer practices per week and then increase the number the closer the team gets to the competition date. This approach has the advantage of allowing more days between each practice round to work on memorization and additional research that is more likely to be needed in the early stages of argument preparation. For example, in a four-week practice schedule, a team might practice twice per week for the first two weeks, then three times per week for the third week, and four times the week before competition.

---

[18] Part of scheduling will also include reserving rooms within your law school.
[19] The purpose of team meetings is discussed below.

2. Judges

Once the schedule is set, it is time to start recruiting volunteer judges. Try to select judges with a variety of backgrounds. Judges should include practitioners, faculty members, and local judges. Also consider including law students, particularly those who have participated in moot court competitions. Former competitors will have insights into moot court competitions that practitioners, judges, and faculty may lack.

Similarly, because competitions typically include judges with varying areas of expertise, recruit practice judges who likewise have varying degrees of familiarity with the legal issues being argued. Although it may be tempting to rely on judges who have expertise in the argument's subject matter, volunteer judges who know nothing of the subject matter can be invaluable in preparing advocates to articulate the arguments more clearly and with less jargon. Furthermore, judges with little subject matter exposure will ask questions with answers that may seem obvious to an expert, but which nonetheless student advocates will need practice articulating. On the other hand, some students may fear being questioned by judges with subject-matter expertise, believing those judges' questions will be more difficult. Do not give in to that fear. Instead, recruit judges who will strongly challenge the advocates' arguments—because practice with the hard questions is essential to prepare for competition. Ideally, by the time of competition, each team will have had the opportunity to answer any question likely to be posed in the competition itself.

Variety also includes recruiting judges with varying personal benching styles. Some judges will ask more information-seeking questions; others will ask more adversarial ones. Some judges may seem antagonistic, while others will seem reserved and hesitant to disrupt with a question. Some judges may pound the bench, demanding an answer when one is not provided; others will simply and quietly move on. Successful practice arguments will include a variety of judging styles, so that the advocates may learn how to respond effectively regardless of the judging style.

Before scheduling specific times for each judge, consider how to best use the judging resources for more effective practice rounds. In the beginning of practice, it may make sense to use more nonexpert judges who can help advocates articulate the answers to more basic questions. Experts are best used in the early and middle stages to increase the degree of difficulty of questioning as the advocates' knowledge increases. Experts can often reveal flaws in an argument that may be missed by other judges. Realizing these mistakes early on allows the team time to adapt the arguments to avoid or at least respond to that flow.

Furthermore, competitions can include benches that are "cold"—where judges ask few, if any, questions—and those that are "hot"—where judges pepper advocates with a seemingly-endless stream of questions.

Advocates should be prepared to handle either type of bench. To accomplish that, attempt to schedule volunteer judges based on their questioning style to ensure that advocates have an opportunity to encounter both cold and hot benches. If it is not possible to arrange the schedule in that manner, ask judges to create either a cold or hot bench. For instance, ask judges to refrain from asking questions to create a cold bench. To facilitate a hot bench, provide judges with a list of suggested questions to ask—this may help with those judges who tend to ask few questions.

Regardless of the type of bench, it is advisable to help prepare all volunteers for their roles as judges. Because the volunteers have busy lives, do not expect them to read the record and each team's brief. Instead, provide the judges with a bench brief that outlines the facts and legal issues before the court. At a minimum, the bench brief should include:

- A list of the key facts relied on in the arguments
- The legal issues before the court
- Summaries of the primary arguments for each side
- Summaries of the key cases and authorities
- Sample questions

It is most helpful if this information is organized by appellant/petitioner and appellee/respondent, and further divided by the two primary legal issues. The bench brief should be just that—brief. Approximately ten pages will typically suffice. The competition briefs and record should also be provided to the judges, but with the understanding that the bench brief will likely be their primary source of information about the arguments.

In addition to the bench brief, prime the judges with information that will help their judging be more productive for the team. For instance, ask judges to focus on a certain legal point or to ask certain questions that the advocates may be struggling to respond to. If a team member is struggling with answering questions directly, ask the judges to press that advocate for answers. Let the judges know where in the practice/preparation process the team is—a team's first practice should have different expectations of preparedness than the dress rehearsal. Telling the judges before a practice round where the team is in the process can help the judge calibrate her questions and tone to match reasonable expectations. Finally, because feedback is part of most oral argument practices, inform the judges of any special concerns they should focus on in providing feedback. To facilitate uniform feedback, consider providing the judges with a feedback checklist or rubric to guide their comments. That rubric can be tailored to each practice round to focus on any particular challenges faced by the team in preparation. For instance, if an advocate is having difficulty remembering to cite cases, highlight that for the judge by including it in the checklist or rubric.[20]

Perhaps the most critical time to prime the judges is the final dress rehearsal. This final practice round before the competition is the time to boost the team's confidence. This final practice is not the time to start pursuing new lines of argument or to undertake new lines of research. Thus, avoid scheduling subject-matter experts to judge the dress rehearsal. While experts can be especially helpful during earlier rounds, at this point you do not want to increase the difficulty of questions because it is too late for the team to do additional research. Similarly, judges who may be especially critical in their feedback can undermine the team's confidence, and are best avoided for the final dress rehearsal. Regardless of the judges scheduled, be sure to let the judges know that this is the final practice before the competition and that the teams will need to maintain their confidence.

3. Questions: Responses and Springboards

Practice rounds will be invaluable in helping to anticipate questions during the competition. Ideally, a team will have enough practice rounds so that nearly every avenue of inquiry has been covered by the time of competition. Nevertheless, advocates should prepare for practice rounds by anticipating potential questions from practice benchers. Before every practice, meet as a team and brainstorm potential questions that may be asked. To get started, each team member should write out 10 to 15 questions to ask her or his teammate. Work through these questions and determine what your answers to them will be. Consider what further questions those answers will prompt and work through those answers as well. Review your argument outline and try to anticipate when a question might arise. Similarly, consider how a given response can be crafted to allow you to resume your argument after providing the judge with an answer.

In many ways, oral argument is just like a first-year law school class—a response to one question almost never settles the matter. Instead, the answer is used as fodder for the next question. That seems daunting for first-year students, but this is what legal analysis and legal conversations are all about. Oral arguments are simply legal analysis between judges and lawyers working to arrive at some solution to a legal quandary. Thus, during practice rounds, the team member who is not arguing should make notes of what questions were asked by the judges and the judges' reactions to the answers given. As a team, use the time

---

[20] For a sample rubric, see below.

between practices to formulate more complete responses to any answer that left a judge unsatisfied. Regardless of the judge's reaction, consider what other questions might flow from those answers. This exercise will help advocates prepare to answer similar questions in future practice rounds. But just as importantly, imagining future questions allows advocates to consider how they may spring-board from an answer to a point the advocate wishes to advance, or to return more seamlessly to the outline of the argument.

4. Processing Feedback

Receiving feedback on your performance can be a bruising experience. It is easy to interpret all feedback as criticism and to take it as a personal affront. No one volunteers to sit through hours-long practices, typically scheduled at odd times at the end of a work day, out of a desire to criticize. Consider that someone who volunteers to judge a moot court practice round is giving a gift of their time and their intellect. A volunteer judge's feedback is his attempt to help the team improve its persuasive and reasoning skills.

With that in mind, advocates should welcome feedback from judges and use it to improve their performance. Take notes of the judge's impressions—both expressing praise and noting areas for improvement. Thank the judges for providing you with their perspective and for their time. Following the practice round, meet as a team and review the judges' feedback. Consider what you might do to improve in response to any legitimate criticism. Just as importantly, consider what prompted the judges' praise. Use that information to acknowledge your own strengths and to consider how you might best capitalize upon them. For instance, if a judge notes that an advocate has a more relaxed demeanor when responding to questions, consider how to transfer that demeanor to the other parts of the argument.

No matter the nature of the feedback you are given, do not argue with the practice round judges. The tendency to defend oneself is natural, but it is unhelpful when feedback is so essential to learning.[21] Some feedback will be conflicting—one judge may dislike the team's argument theme, another may find it compelling. Nevertheless, that conflict does not make one judge right and one judge wrong. Rather, any judge providing feedback is responding based on her own experience, perspective, personal style, and preferences. In that way, feedback should be viewed as valuable information for the team about how its

---

[21]Furthermore, teams that repeatedly argue with judges' feedback gain a troublesome reputation, which decreases the likelihood of recruiting volunteer judges.

arguments are perceived by others. That information is useful in gauging what reaction it wishes to prompt in advancing its arguments. For instance, it could be appropriate to have a theme that shocks a judge if the case involves shocking facts. Nevertheless, if judges repeatedly have similarly negative reactions to an argument, theme, question response, or advocate's demeanor, that will help identify the most obvious areas for improvement.

To facilitate consistent feedback, consider providing judges with a feedback checklist or rubric. If your competition makes available the rubric used by competition judges to score competition rounds, use that form to ask for feedback during practice rounds, if doing so is permitted by the competition rules. Otherwise, create your own rubric that focuses on specific concerns. Below is a sample of an argument feedback form that can be tailored for that purpose.

SAMPLE ORAL ARGUMENT
FEEDBACK CHECKLIST

Student Name:_____

Arguing for Appellant/Petitioner or Appellee/Respondent

Respect for panel	Excellent	Acceptable	Unacceptable
Organization of argument	Excellent	Acceptable	Unacceptable
Gestures; eye contact, etc.	Excellent	Acceptable	Unacceptable
Theme/Theory of case	Excellent	Acceptable	Unacceptable
Answers to questions 1	Excellent	Acceptable	Unacceptable
2	Excellent	Acceptable	Unacceptable
3	Excellent	Acceptable	Unacceptable
4	Excellent	Acceptable	Unacceptable
5	Excellent	Acceptable	Unacceptable
6	Excellent	Acceptable	Unacceptable
Use of record	Excellent	Acceptable	Unacceptable
Use of authority	Excellent	Acceptable	Unacceptable
Persuasiveness	Excellent	Acceptable	Unacceptable

General comments:
_____
_____
_____
_____
_____
_____
_____

5. Finding Your Voice

Because most competitions prohibit faculty input on brief drafting and oral argument content, students are largely responsible for choosing the direction of their arguments and their own style in delivering those arguments. Consequently, the primary method of delivering feedback—oral argument practice and competition—is properly viewed as a prime opportunity for student-advocates to develop their individual approach to advocacy and to find their own voice. "Voice" is described as an individual advocate's personal style of delivery, point of view, or personality conveyed during oral argument.

The process of receiving and responding to questions and feedback from judges in practice and in competition can make advocates feel unbalanced or uncertain. This is especially true when the questions are difficult or the feedback is conflicting or contradictory. When receiving feedback, it can be easy to lose sight of your own strengths and individual advocacy style.[22] Some judges will have opinions of your style. Take such opinions with a grain of salt. Style is often a matter of personal tastes and comfort level. Thus, it may be necessary to disregard a judge's critique that requires a fundamental altering of who you are such that it forces you to assume an unnatural or deceptive persona. Indeed, adopting an unnatural style could undermine your advocacy as your will appear less genuine to the bench during competition. Some judges will respond to your arguments in unanticipated ways. Nevertheless, oral argument is a unique opportunity to hear how individuals of varying backgrounds and expertise receive your arguments and respond to your delivery. At the end of the day, each student has the choice to adopt or reject any judge's recommendation based on individual preference and style.

There is no one correct way to succeed at oral argument. Different advocates will have different strengths and preferences in presenting their arguments. Some advocates will feel comfortable taking a dramatic or even fiery approach to advocacy. Others will feel more comfortable with a more moderate or relaxed tone. Despite these differences, each advocate's argument can still be equally effective. Indeed, the most effective advocacy is that which is delivered with sincerity and a clear understanding of the client's legal position. For this reason, advocates should strive to remain true to their own personal style while remaining within general professional standards. In short, reject any feedback that would force you into a role or personality that does not suit who you are.

Of course, advocates presenting oral arguments are performing for an audience that has certain expectations regarding dress, decorum, and

---

[22] Which is precisely why it is important to be able to distinguish between good and bad feedback as discussed above.

professional conduct. As such, oral arguments are not intended to be forum for personal opinion and expression. Advocates should not expect to feel as relaxed or casual as they do at home or in a gathering of friends. Use the practice rounds to perfect your argument performance and as a vehicle to establish your voice. Practice your professional identity—e.g., wear appropriate courtroom attire and behave professionally with judges, teammates, and coaches.

Remember, practice rounds are not a rehearsal. Moot court is not about remembering lines of a play. Too much memorization of lines can turn an advocate's delivery into a robotic monotone. By the time of competition you will have made the same arguments multiple times; the trick is to avoid becoming so rote in your delivery that it appears to the court that you have said all of this before. It is acceptable to be a "real" person—to have emotion, to occasionally misspeak or even mispronounce a word. That being said, remember that oral arguments are presented to judges, not to a lay jury. Thus advocates should employ emotional appeals sparingly.

E. TEAM MANAGEMENT AND CONFLICT RESOLUTION STRATEGIES FOR ORAL ARGUMENT

Just as with writing the brief, it is likely that challenges and disagreements will arise during the oral argument practice rounds. In fact, conflicts are perhaps more likely to arise because of the added stress of live performance, being questioned by judges, and occasional ego-bruising feedback. Chapter 3 outlined conflict resolution strategies for teams to employ during brief writing. Those strategies remain relevant in oral argument practice—and in legal practice or any team endeavor. In addition to reviewing the tips provided above,[23] below are some ideas to keep in mind to maintain team cohesion and deal with conflicts with particular respect to oral argument.

First, every team member should start with the assumption that all members of the team are equally smart, dedicated, and hardworking. When we assume the best motivations and intentions for others, it can help us change our own reactions. For instance, if a team member is not performing to expectations and we are assuming they are honestly trying their best, it forces us to look for a solution. That is, we look for reasons they are struggling with the material or their articulation of it, and we devise solutions to those struggles.

Second, consider the judges' feedback as generally applicable to everyone on the team. While it might be directed at one team member on a

---

[23] See *supra* 37-40.

particular day, it is likely that on a different day it will be relevant to the other team member. Many of the challenges presented in oral argument are universal—even if they are not synchronous. For instance, a judge may criticize an advocate for failing to directly answer a question posed. In all likelihood, the other member of the team has made the same error before or will in the future. Thus, consider the feedback and suggestions with respect to how they can improve your performance, even if they are directed at your teammate. This is especially important to keep in mind if the feedback is lopsided—so that one team member receives more criticism than the other. When on the receiving end of positive feedback, stay humble.

Third, as noted above, some competitions permit teams to split argument times according to team preference. This division can be a source of tension if both advocates are focused more on their own individual opportunity to argue instead of the team success. Be flexible to adjusting the split of time between arguments, keeping in mind that the goal is to succeed as a team. If your teammate's argument is more compelling or more complex, it may make sense to allocate slightly more time to it for the sake of delivering the most compelling argument for the purposes of competition. That being said, if the team decides that yours is the argument that deserves more time, do not permit the time to become so lopsided that your teammate does not have an opportunity to shine as well. In addition to undermining your teammate, such a strategy would likely backfire if the judges are unable to adequately assess both team members' performance for the purposes of scoring. Ideally, moot court practice and competition will permit both advocates to share the opportunity to master oral argument skills while still achieving success as a team.

Similarly, tensions can arise as the team decides what issues to rebut and who will deliver the rebuttal. Devise a system to reach a decision on these issues. Always consider the views of your teammates, especially on what issue to rebut, as each member will have primary expertise on her or his particular argument. For instance, if one team member will always deliver the rebuttal, agree to that person having the final say in what issue is argued in that rebuttal. That does not mean the non-rebutting team member has no say about what points should be covered in rebuttal. Rather, it means that both teammates must recognize that there will be only a few seconds to decide in the heat of the competition so that one person must have the final word to avoid delaying the rebuttal or delivering a laundry list of topics because the team could not reach consensus. Deciding on who has the final say can prevent conflict—and delay—during competition.

Finally, to best manage team conflicts, schedule weekly team meetings to address any concerns. Set a regular schedule that allows the advocates and coaches to touch base. This will provide a natural opportunity to discuss any concerns about the practices, arguments, or work-load. These meetings should be separate from oral argument practice rounds. Right after a practice, stress and emotions may be running too high to productively resolve any conflicts or concerns. Instead, schedule the meetings on days when there is not a practice round. Just as with brief writing, if there are issues that cannot be resolved between team members, invite your faculty or student coach to facilitate dialogue.

CHAPTER 4
TIPS AND TAKEAWAYS

- Memorize the key facts from the record.

- Memorize the key cases critical to the arguments.

- Develop a welcoming attitude for constructive feedback and criticism.

- Incorporate feedback into your argument.

- Stay flexible to the flow of the oral argument discussion.

- Find your own personal advocacy style.

- Practice, practice, practice.

CHAPTER 5
THE COMPETITION

From team selection to competition results, the entire moot court process is an educational experience. Much of the energy during the moot court process is focused on preparation for the competition. Each aspect of the competition offers opportunities to learn practical skills that will be useful to your career.

As diligent as you have been with your preparation, the competition may still be a nerve-wracking experience. This chapter shares some practical tips to manage the various aspects of the competition process to help you maximize your moot court experience.

A. PRACTICAL CONSIDERATIONS

Once your team has registered for the competition, review the competition schedule. The schedule will include not only the start time of each competition day, but details about the number of argument rounds and when those rounds will take place. A hard copy of the schedule may be mailed to registered teams, or a digital copy may be posted on the competition website.[1]

Refer to the schedule as you arrange for travel and lodging. For intraschool moot court competitions,[2] you will be familiar with the amount of

---

[1] Some parts of the competition website may be password protected. Be sure that your travel packet includes password information so that you have access to the competition website when traveling.
[2] "Intraschool" competitions refer to moot court competitions hosted at your law school with participants only from your law school.

time it takes you to get to the law school, where to park, and what room to go to. For interschool moot court competitions,[3] some travel will be required. You will thus be in what is likely an unfamiliar setting. Take care of the practical aspects of the competition to avoid unnecessary distraction and stress. Work with your school's administrator as soon as you register for the competition to plan travel. Competitions are typically scheduled over several days, and this doesn't include travel days. Double check the dates and time commitments of the competition so you don't miss competition day check-in. When you are making travel arrangements, plan to stay for the duration of the competition. The final round of the competition is often one of the only competition rounds open to spectators. Plan to attend the final round. Seeing the final round is a good way to cap the competition experience. When traveling, of course, allow time for delays—whether at the airport or on the road. The schedule of moot court competition is rigid. You don't want to miss a minute!

As part of your travel planning, also make arrangements to handle your scholastic commitments. Confirm attendance policies for classes, and work with the professor if any documentation relating to your absences will be required. Arrange for a classmate to share her or his class notes for missed classes. Confirm that all course work, including assigned reading, is completed and, if necessary, submitted before you travel.

In general, all competitions will have preliminary rounds, where each team will have the opportunity to argue at least twice. One argument will be "on brief," meaning the team will be arguing the same side as their written brief. The other argument will be "off brief," meaning that the team will be arguing for the side not argued by the brief. (But, of course, the team will have practiced oral arguments on both sides.) Depending on the structure of the competition, the preliminary rounds may be scheduled within a short period of time that requires back-to-back arguments, or may be scheduled over multiple days.

Typically, once the preliminary rounds are completed, scores are tabulated with only a set number of teams progressing to the next round. At that point, the field of teams is reduced in each subsequent round until two teams advance to compete against each other in the final round of the competition. As the competition progresses, the time between rounds is often compressed.

Upon arriving at the competition, you will receive the detailed competition schedule for your team. Review the schedule, because the detailed competition schedule may vary from previously mailed or posted

---

[3]"Interschool" competitions refer to moot court competitions hosted at another law school with participants from law schools around the country.

schedules. You want to determine the date, time, and location of your scheduled arguments. Allow time to check the location of the rooms where you will be arguing, rooms where announcements will be made (or posted), restrooms, and vending machines. Review the schedule to confirm when you are "on brief" and when you are "off brief." Remember, the time between rounds may be limited. Each round may be located in different rooms—or even buildings. The date, time, and location of rooms assigned for the rounds beyond the preliminary rounds may not be announced until the completion of the preliminary rounds. Confirm where and when this information will be announced or posted so that you know exactly where you need to be.

With the competition schedule in hand, time to get into character. The moot court competition is more than knowing the law, the policy considerations, and the facts. The moot court competition is a performance. As you get ready to argue, get into character. Even veteran Broadway performers have to get into character before a show. Preparation is key. Refresh your memory by reviewing your oral argument outline, reciting your introduction, and even taking a sample question from your teammate.

Getting into character isn't just about being confident in what you are going to say; getting into character also means dressing for the part. Deliberate, informed choices in what to wear translates into confidence during the competition. When making clothing choices, recognize the assumptions that the audience may make about your clothing choices. Dressing professionally minimizes the risk of these unnecessary distractions. Typically, dressing professionally for a lawyer means wearing a suit, preferably in a dark color. In selecting your suit, consider fit and any distracting accessories. Constantly tugging an errant collar or smoothing a wayward lapel can distract you, your teammate, and the judges. Most competition rules require you to avoid revealing your school affiliation during the length of the competition. Thus, you should leave the school logo shirts, ties, pens, notepads, cups, and backpacks at the hotel.

While you will be wearing a suit, you should still dress comfortably. You may be dashing across the university campus to get to the next competition round. You will be standing on your feet for many hours of each day. You'll be sitting, standing, and walking throughout the course of the competition. Consequently, avoid overly restrictive clothing, as well as shoes that pinch or cause blisters, or that are difficult to walk in.

Competition day (or days, depending on the competition schedule) will be exhilarating but tiring. Every minute of your time is going to be scheduled. Plan to remain at the competition site throughout the competition day. That means you should bring supplies. You don't want to spend precious time during the competition trying to locate a vending machine with bottled water that takes dollar bills, a safety pin to temporarily fix a hem, an aspirin to squash a headache, or an umbrella to dash between buildings on a rainy day. It may sound like basic advice, but pack a competition day bag that includes the following items:

➢ mints/cough drops
➢ water bottles
➢ low-sugar snacks such as protein bars
➢ tissues
➢ spot cleaner
➢ hair brush
➢ lint brush
➢ adhesive bandages
➢ aspirin
➢ safety pins
➢ pens
➢ pads of paper
➢ competition schedule
➢ change for vending machine
➢ umbrella
➢ extra pair of panty hose/tights

During your time at the competition, identify one aspect of the oral argument that you would repeat in a future oral argument, and identify one aspect of the argument that you would alter for a future argument. This self-reflection helps keep you engaged with your performance at the competition and thinking about how to transfer this experience to the future.

B. PROFESSIONALISM

Civility in the practice of law starts in law school. Although passion about arguments and persuasive phrasing is part of the moot court competition, keep the behavior before, during, and after the competition rounds civil. Heckling, staring contests, and whisper campaigns don't belong in the moot court competition (or in the practice of law, for that matter). Respectfully engage with the other competitors throughout the entire competition. Greet the other team before going into the competition room. Shake hands afterwards. You know how hard you worked to be prepared for the competition. The other teams have worked hard too.

You are representing not only your team but also your academic institution. Nerves can be frayed during the heat of competition, but try to maintain an even temper. No matter what the perceived outrage is, shouting matches and profanity have no place at a moot court competition (or in the practice of law). Let the work speak for itself and refrain from theatrics. Keep in mind that competition judges are often local practitioners or judges or members of the local bar. You not only want to be respectful of those who have volunteered their time, but also to consider the networking opportunity. While you shouldn't try to turn the moot court competition into a job interview, be aware that the legal community is small. There's only one chance to make a first impression. Don't let the stress of the competition undermine your professionalism or your reputation in your legal community.

C. MANAGING STRESS

Butterflies in the stomach are a part of any competition. During your law school career, you have probably developed various mechanisms for dealing with stress. Preparation—and over-preparation—is the best strategy for overcoming stress. And much of that preparation you have completed by the day of competition. Your careful construction of the appellate brief and attention to oral argument practices will make you comfortable with the material, increasing your confidence and minimizing your anxiety. Nevertheless, no matter how much you have practiced and prepared, nerves are a part of any performance. (And oral argument really is a performance.) Below is a list of strategies to help you manage that stress.

1. Eat your breakfast. Get a good night's sleep before the competition and eat a healthy breakfast. Try not to have high amounts of sugar or caffeine before the competition. Rumbling stomachs and caffeine jitters will exacerbate stress.

2. Map out the competition rooms. Running late or being unable to locate the room is only going to increase your stress levels. After you receive the detailed competition schedule, locate each assigned room. Determine the best way to access each assigned room and the amount of time you need to arrive at each assigned room on time.

3. Active visualization. Seeing is believing. Well, at least visualizing can help calm your nerves. As you are waiting to enter the assigned competition room, close your eyes for 30 seconds. Picture yourself walking into the room, acknowledging the other team, nodding to the timekeeper, and sitting at the designated counsel table. Picture yourself rising as the judges walk into the room. Picture yourself moving to the podium, opening your notes, and resting your hands comfortably on the podium. Picture yourself making the arguments, using the legally accurate and yet persuasive phrasing that you have been practicing, and handling the judges' questions in a complete manner. Picture yourself reciting your conclusion, thanking the panel of judges, and resuming your seat at the counsel table. Then picture yourself shaking the hands of the timekeeper, the other team, and the judges. Picture yourself walking out of the room. This may seem a little bit silly. But seeing yourself in the experience can help quiet nerves.

4. Take a deep breath. Ever been nervous and started to feel dizzy? Chances are, you may have unintentionally restricted oxygen flow to your body. When stressed, we may hold our breath or take only short, shallow breaths. This starves the body and brain of oxygen. After your active visualization exercise and before entering the competition room, take a series of deep breaths. Don't forget to take a deep breath as you walk to the podium. As you stand at the podium, assume a formal, yet relaxed posture. And don't lock your knees. Stand straight, but keep the knees relaxed. Also avoid clenching your shoulders or hunching over the podium. These positions are sometimes considered to be problematic because the positions may restrict blood flow and may produce dizziness. Even if these positions don't cause dizziness, they can produce muscle fatigue. Physical stress on the body through shallow breaths or clenched body posture will increase your emotional stress levels.

5. Be in the moment. While you are waiting to argue, and even during the argument, lots of thoughts will pass through your mind. Try not to think about the upcoming rounds or the law school classes you are missing while attending the competition. You have worked hard to gain a mastery of the issues, authorities, and facts. The competition rounds are going to be a series of informed conversations. This is your chance to shine. Enjoy!

D. PROCESSING THE COMPETITION EXPERIENCE AND THE COMPETITION RESULTS

The competition may feel like the culmination of your efforts, but the competition doesn't mark the end of the educational experience. Every team, even the team that wins the competition, needs to process the competition experience and evaluate the competition results. This is a key part of the educational process. Evaluating past experiences informs future decisions. For example, the decisions about this competition will directly inform your experience in future moot court competitions—whether as a competitor or student coach. Moreover, evaluating this past experience will promote the application of the lessons learned to your experiences as an intern, extern, summer associate, or attorney. In other words, evaluating the moot court experience will have immediate and future benefits.

POST-COMPETITION REFLECTIONS

When you return from the competition, reflect upon the entire moot court experience. Consider the following:

1. Which, if any, of the three personal goals that you identified in Chapter 1 of this book have you accomplished? How did you achieve those goal(s)?

_____

_____

_____

_____

_____

_____

2. Which, if any, of the three personal goals that you identified in Chapter 1 of this book did you not accomplish? Why did you not achieve those goal(s)?

_____

_____

_____

_____

_____

_____

3. Given your experience from team selection to competition results, what goal(s) would you alter, discard, or add? Why?

_____

_____

_____

_____

_____

_____

WORKSHEET

4. What was the most surprising aspect of the moot court experience? Be specific.

   _____

   _____

   _____

   _____

   _____

   _____

5. Considering the entire moot court experience, what do you know now that you wished you knew at the beginning of the experience? Explain your response.

   _____

   _____

   _____

   _____

   _____

   _____

The competition scores will typically identify the score for each oral argument round and brief. This may arrive a few days after the competition concludes, or a few months later. Once you have the scores, schedule a time to discuss the scores with your teammates and coaches.

When reviewing the oral argument scores, consider how you assessed your performances during the competition and how you assess your performances now. Identify one aspect of the performance that you would change. Identify one aspect of the performance that you would continue to practice in the future. Then review the score sheet to see how the scores and comments (if any are provided) compare to your own assessment.

When reviewing the brief score, begin with your own assessment of the brief. Review an unmarked copy of your final brief. If you were to rewrite the brief, what would you change? Identify at least three aspects of the brief that could be revised. If you were to refer to the brief as a model for the future, what aspects of the brief would you use as a model? Identify at least three aspects of the brief that you would use as a model. Then review the score sheet for the brief to see if the scores and comments (if any are provided) compare to your own assessment.

Moot court is more than a competition. Moot court is a transformative educational experience. No matter the results of the competition, if you learned something during the process, you have succeeded!

CHAPTER 5
TIPS AND TAKEAWAYS

- After registering for the competition, review the competition schedule.

- Make all travel and lodging arrangements when you register for the competition.

- Before each argument round, get into character.

- No matter what happens, be respectful and civil.

- Manage your stress with preparation, visualization, and breathing.

- Enjoy the competition!

- After the competition, reflect upon the experience.

A

Appellate brief
    action plan: 33-47
    checklist: 25-28, 41, 80, 81, 83-86
    conclusion: 50, 51, 61, 67, 72
    grammar and style: 38, 40, 80, 81, 85, 86
    logistics: 39, 40, 41
    narrative: 51-59
    point headings: 40, 66-71, 72-73
    research: 13, 17, 18, 19
    Question Presented: 24, 40, 52, 60-66, 67, 68
    Statement of the Case: 52
    Statement of the Facts: 24, 40, 51-59
    Summary of the Argument: 40, 51, 68, 72-73
    Table of Authorities: 81, 82, 83
    Table of Contents: 66, 69, 80, 82, 83
    theme: 18, 24, 40, 50, 51, 60, 68, 72, 80
    theory of the case: 2, 40, 50, 51, 80

Authorities. *See also* research
    uses: 49, 73, 98, 104, 111, 112, 114, 121
    weight of authority: 73, 111

C

Citation: 24, 25, 28, 38, 49, 72, 81-82, 97, 111, 112, 113, 114, 116, 122

F

Formatting, argument: 23, 89-91, 97, 102

Formatting, brief: 24, 25, 27, 67, 68, 69, 80-86

M

Moot court competition
    etiquette: 26, 127-128, 133, 134-135. *See also* professionalism
    logistics: 37-41, 89-91, 112-115, 131-134
    managing stress: 3, 30, 39, 40, 110, 128-130, 132, 135-136
    professionalism: 39, 40, 81, 127, 128, 133, 134-135
    record: 18-20, 23, 94, 96, 97, 98, 112, 121, 125, 130
    reflections on: 134, 136-139
    rules: 11, 19, 23-30, 38, 40, 49, 52, 69, 73, 79, 80-83, 90, 92, 93, 110, 115, 124, 133

O

Oral argument. *See also* Oral argument practices
    action plan: 92-115
    advocacy: 20, 21-22, 93-94, 107, 118
    argument: 98-102
    case facts: 96-98
    closing: 95-96

    concessions: 107-108
    drafting arguments: 92-93
    opening: 95-96
    points of conflict: 102-106
    question types: 103
    rebuttal: 29, 91, 93, 96, 108, 109, 110, 115, 129
    responding to questions: 97, 102-106, 109, 112, 113, 114, 116, 120-121, 122-123, 127
    role of the record: 94, 96, 97, 98, 112, 121, 125, 130
    rules: 90, 92, 93, 110, 115, 124, 133
    springboarding: 122-123
    structure: 23, 89-91, 97, 102
    style, advocate: 127-128
    style, judge: 120, 121, 123
    sur-rebuttal: 30, 91, 93, 110

Oral argument practices
    action plan: 92-93
    appearance/clothing: 128, 133
    body language/gestures: 94, 128
    conflict resolution: 105-106, 128-130
    critique/feedback: 123-124
    dress rehearsal: 122
    getting into character: 133
    judges: 120-122
    off brief: 101
    research role: 115-118
    rubric/checklist: 125
    schedule/scheduling: 119

Organization
    generally: 73-74
    IRAC: 73-74
    paragraphing: 74
    thesis sentences: 74. *See also* topic sentences
    topic sentences: 74

P

Persuasion: 5-6, 18-20, 25, 33, 47, 50, 73-75, 80, 82, 93, 96-98, 101-102, 111, 118

Professionalism: 26, 39, 40, 81, 127, 128, 133, 134-135

Proofreading: 79-86

Q

Quotations: 76, 82

R

Research: 13, 18-19, 25, 49-50, 94, 115-118

S

Standard of review: 13, 35, 60

Style
    gender inclusive language: 75
    level of formality: 76
    nominalization: 76
    pronouns: 75
    tone: 61, 76
    voice, active and passive: 75
    wordiness: 76-78

W
Writing process
    collaboration: 2-3, 34, 37-41
    conflict resolution: 38-40, 44
    sample schedule: 41